For my husband—
for being my best friend, and
for believing in what the Lord is calling me to do.

For my sisters in Christ—
for showing me godly friendships, and
for every word of encouragement about this study.

A special thanks to the Engram family—
for showing me how to follow Jesus and study His Word!

D1568556

CONTENTS

A SON'S LAST WORDS

In 2008, I thought I had it all.

In the picture below, you can see that. I had an amazing husband and two crazy boys. I was an attorney with a fancy office in an international law firm. I loved living in Arizona and driving around with the top down in my red convertible. You get the picture. Sounds like I really did have it all, right? I thought so too, until April 25, 2008. On that morning, our three-year-old, Austin, who had been sick with strep throat, never woke up. There was nothing anyone could have done. Austin was gone.

My perfect world came crashing down. I realized that I had nothing and had achieved nothing because I had no relationship with God. He had no part of my life. I realized *everything* could be taken away at any moment—even my husband and my children.

But even though I had ignored God most of my life, He stepped in to save me. He used losing Austin to call me to a different life. A few days after Austin died, I gave my life to Jesus. I acknowledged Him as my Savior and made Him Lord of my life. A friend gave me my first Bible, and my journey began as a Christ follower.

Losing Austin led me to the Bible and the magnificent truths contained in it. When you lose someone, it seems like you can always remember your last moments together. My last words to Austin and his last words to me are burned in my heart and mind like nothing else. He woke me up in the middle of the night and said, "Mom, I want to brush my teeth. And my throat hurts." He was so mature for his age and he talked like such a big boy. So we got up and went into the bathroom. He brushed his teeth and I got his medicine.

As I settled him back into his bed, I made him drink some water. He was moaning and he pulled back because his throat hurt so much (even after more than forty-eight hours on antibiotics). I said, "I know it hurts, angel, but you have to drink it. Your body needs it to get better." He bravely took another swallow, still moaning.

"You are one tough cookie," I said as I smoothed the hair on his forehead.

"I'm a tough cookie?" he asked with his little blond head tilted to one side (as if to say, silly mom, cookies are not tough!).

Smiling, I explained, "Tough cookie means that you are brave and strong." He nodded and gave me a big grin and confirmed, "I *am* a tough cookie!"

"Yes, you are. Now, back to bed," I said as he curled back up with his "boo" (his blanket).

As I tucked him in, I told him, "You're going to start feeling better tomorrow. The medicine is going to start working and you are going to be better tomorrow." I kissed his head and turned off the light. "Love you."

"Love you," Austin murmured back as he cuddled in his bed.

Although I remain brokenhearted with the loss of Austin, I am grateful for our last words of love and the clever, funny little boy the Lord gave us for three years.

As I began to study the Bible, the gospel of John gripped my heart because it contains the last words Jesus said to His disciples. As a new believer and grieving mom, I pored over and over these words. Jesus knew these were His final hours. Jesus knew these would be the last words He would speak to His disciples before

His death. Oh, what I would have given to know that night when I tucked him into bed that those were to be my final moments with Austin!

Since Jesus did know what were His final moments with His disciples, I wanted to know what He said. After studying John 13–17, I am certain Jesus taught lessons in those last hours that He especially wanted to imprint on them.

Jesus' last words changed my life. I believe His words have the power to change yours.

Through this study we will also catch a glimpse of the apostle John, who is widely presumed to be the disciple "whom Jesus loved." In our culture, it might be said that John was one of Jesus' best friends. After spending three years with Jesus, you might assume that all the disciples stood by Jesus through His arrest, trial, and crucifixion. But the disciples scattered—except John. John was the only one of the Twelve recorded as being at the cross.

John stood by his friend and Lord, risking everything to see his friend to the end. John's loyalty stirred my heart to find out more. I learned that this apostle was often with Jesus when He performed amazing miracles. He was there when Jesus commanded Lazarus back to life after four days in a tomb. John was there when Jesus was transfigured on the Mount of Olives, and he was there in the garden of Gethsemane when Jesus prayed and agonized over what was to come. In fact, Jesus loved John so much that He entrusted the care of His mother, Mary, to him in the last moments before His death.

Through this study, you will read what John had to say about Jesus. You will experience Jesus through John's eyes. Who better to show you the heart of Jesus than one of His best friends? In this gospel, John shared the intimacy of Christ's final hours with His disciples.

While it was John's loyalty and friendship that intrigued me to learn more, it was the words of Jesus in these chapters that amazed me, humbled me, and changed me. Consider this: if you knew that you only had hours left on this earth, what would you say to your friends and loved ones? Would you try to tell them how much you love them? Would you try to impart last words of wisdom? Would you share your innermost heart with them?

▸ **Our changed lives are meant to bring glory to God.**

You will discover that Jesus did all these things during His final hours with the disciples and in His final prayer. Through this study, I hope you experience a new revelation of the amazing love of our God and gain a deeper understanding of the heart of Jesus. When you begin to see more of Him, you begin to examine your own heart and life. During this study, I was repeatedly overwhelmed by His love and lifted up and amazed by His promises. God's Word is so powerful to change our lives!

While God does want us to draw closer to Him and transform our lives through His Word, His goal is not only about changing us "on the inside." Our changed lives are meant to bring glory to God. As you study the gospel of John, you will discover that God wants you to love others so that all may believe in Jesus and have eternal life with Him. In fact, John stated this as the purpose of his gospel: "that you may believe that Jesus is the Christ, the Son of God, and that believing you may have life in his name" (John 20:31).

It is my prayer that you dive deep into the heart of Jesus and allow His lovingkindness to change your heart. I pray that you emerge from this study determined to live a life that shows the world around you the amazing love of God.

Thank you for allowing me the privilege of sharing this journey with you. Let's get started!

Prayerfully,

Kim

GETTING THE MOST FROM THIS STUDY

Allowing the Holy Spirit and the Word of God to work in your heart takes time.

To allow more time for reflection, each week consists of just four lessons. For each daily lesson, first read the assigned passage in your own Bible to get the overall context. Next, the assigned Scripture for the day is provided, verse by verse, in this book. Beside each verse is space to write what the words reveal to us about God— something about the Father, Son, or the Holy Spirit.

Journal in the chart for each lesson as the Holy Spirit guides you. It is important that you do not feel you have to write something in every space. Studying these chapters verse by verse is an exercise in reflecting and seeking understanding. If nothing comes to mind, leave the spaces blank. One caution, however, is to take care that you do not go so fast through the verses that you do not allow time to let the Holy Spirit speak to you.

On the fifth day each week, you'll find questions for reviewing, reflecting, and praying about the daily lessons. A discussion guide follows each week, to work through with a small group, though you may also do this study on your own. But I encourage you to go through this material with at least one other person because it will deepen your understanding of the Scriptures and hold you accountable for making changes in your life that reflect *His Last Words*.

To make your Bible study time more meaningful and impactful, visit **MoodyPublishersWomen.com** for a free digital study pack for this Bible study. If you have any questions, please do not hesitate to contact me at **KimErickson@LoveMyWord.com** or **www.LoveMyWord.com**. I'd love to hear from you!

WEEK ONE

love
one another

JOHN 13

Our study begins with this beautiful picture painted by John, starting in chapter 13, verse 1:

> Now before the Feast of the Passover, when Jesus knew that his hour had come to depart out of this world to the Father, having loved his own who were in the world, he loved them to the end.

Jesus knows that His time with the disciples is drawing to an end. Jesus knows what is about to happen to Him and to His friends. The final hours are upon Him. The enemy is on the way. It is time. Jesus knows He is about to speak—for the last time before His death—with the disciples. He looks around the table at the men He has chosen to change the world. I imagine His heart aches for the pain they will endure for Him, for His name, for the gospel.

He gets up from the table and begins washing their feet—a shocking act in their culture.

When He is finished, He speaks to them more directly than ever before. The time for parables is over. Jesus knows these men must understand, must deeply and thoroughly comprehend, why He has come and why He must die. He must fill their hearts with love and courage!

WEEK 1 | DAY 1

PRIDE AND POSITION

Read John 13:1–11 in your Bible,
then complete the chart below, verse by verse.

Briefly write what each verse reveals to you about the Father, the Son,
or the Holy Spirit. Perhaps the verse reflects a character trait of God
(merciful, patient, gentle, loving). The verse might show what the
Lord values (obedience, service) or how He wants us to behave
(humbly, kindly, compassionately). It's fine to leave some spaces blank
since you won't find an answer to the question in every verse. The idea
is to read each verse thinking, *Does this verse tell me anything about
God?* and then writing what comes to mind.

JOHN 13:1–11	What does this verse tell me about God?
1. Now before the Feast of the Passover, when Jesus knew that his hour had come to depart out of this world to the Father, having loved his own who were in the world, he loved them to the end.	*Sample response:* *Jesus loved His disciples to the end.* *Jesus loves me as His own.* — Being of & from the world, Jesus still loves the disciples. Jesus shows He is God in His knowledge of His final hour - no man knows his time of death.
2. During supper, when the devil had already put it into the heart of Judas Iscariot, Simon's son, to betray him,	
3. Jesus, knowing that the Father had given all things into his hands, and that he had come from God and was going back to God,	Jesus knows all : He is omnipotent + omnipresent

What does this verse tell me about God?

4. rose from supper. He laid aside his outer garments, and taking a towel, tied it around his waist.

Jesus is a willing servant, I must also be willing.

5. Then he poured water into a basin and began to wash the disciples' feet and to wipe them with the towel that was wrapped around him.

Jesus shows His love + His servanthood, not to man but to God.

6. He came to Simon Peter, who said to him, "Lord, do you wash my feet?"

7. Jesus answered him, "What I am doing you do not understand now, but afterward you will understand."

Is Jesus referring to after He dies on the cross + rises again?

8. Peter said to him, "You shall never wash my feet." Jesus answered him, "If I do not wash you, you have no share with me."

If we do not accept Jesus to wash away our sin, we are not of God, but rather against God.

9. Simon Peter said to him, "Lord, not my feet only but also my hands and my head!"

Peter wanted to show that he wanted every part of him to be cleansed and of Jesus.

10. Jesus said to him, "The one who has bathed does not need to wash, except for his feet, but is completely clean. And you are clean, but not every one of you."

11. For he knew who was to betray him; that was why he said, "Not all of you are clean."

God knows all things, even our sin, & things we are yet to do.

If you knew you only had one day to live, with whom would you spend your last hours on earth and why?

I would spend my last hours with loved ones: mom & dad, grammy, Nakahla, Lydia, Vaughn, Caleb, Kaylee, Kelli, Erin, Jesse, Pastor Chamberland, William, Ran Hummel, (& grampy if I could of been able to), Mrs. Crystal

We know how Jesus chose to spend His last hours on earth—with those He loved, and loved "to the end." John gave us some understanding of how Jesus loves us and what He did for us. The word he used for "end" is *telos*, meaning "perfection" or "completeness." Jesus loves His own to perfection. Jesus loves His own to completeness. The love of Jesus makes you complete!

If you knew you only had one day to live, what would you do with your last hours?

Pray, be with my loved ones, tell them I love them, look at everyone of them and study them all. Tell them how they have impacted my life & how happy I am to know they are all saved & going to see me again soon. To keep living & loving on God no matter what life throws at them. I would want to hug everyone, & kiss my family & my hubby {& if I had kids}

I am willing to bet that washing feet did not make your list! But serving one another in love and humility is so important to God that Jesus spent some of His last hours on earth washing the feet of His disciples. Jesus gave us a living, loving, and humble example of how He expects us to love one another.

It is interesting that the disciples did not appear to have any servants. It would have been customary in the culture at the time, at least in wealthier circles, to have a servant wash their feet. The disciples must have done duties themselves, typically performed by servants.[1]

By the time the Last Supper took place, crowds were following Jesus. Surely some of the followers were servants in other households and would have gladly given up their posts to serve Jesus and the disciples. Yet, Jesus had no servants. Doesn't that say something about the character of God? He did not ask servants to attend to Him. More importantly, He did not expect it. Clearly, pride and position mean nothing to God.

In your last hours on earth, what would you tell your loved ones? What lessons would you want them to learn from the example of your life?

Listen to the tap on your shoulder when you're about to do something wrong - that's probably the Holy Spirit knocking,or a loved one looking for you.
Don't be afraid to lose in life, for when you lose, you will gain back more time, more love, or just more > in due time as God sees fit.

Next, Peter objected when it was his turn to have his feet washed. "You can't wash *my* feet!" But Jesus' reply to Peter was startling; that if He didn't wash him, Peter would have no part in Him. Jesus has illustrated both humbly serving one another and the spiritual aspect to His act: in order to share in fellowship and eternal life we must be cleansed through Jesus. When we put our faith in Christ, we are cleansed—forgiven and made children of God.

Jesus told the disciples that, by the grace of God alone, they would one day share in God's kingdom. What are you holding on to that might be keeping you from fully sharing in your inheritance as a follower of Christ? Are you feeling guilty

about something that is keeping you from joyfully sharing in God's grace? Write
about it here: My sin holds me back. When I fail, & sin, it is hard for me to get back from where I started. Course God helps me & I need Him to help me, but I am often stubborn & get in my own way. Of course being stubborn & not repenting is also sin. I just need to be so close to God, so "in" with His footsteps, that when I fall, I can find His path again.

Ask God to forgive you and know that you are completely clean through the grace of Christ!

The washing of the disciples' feet also is symbolic of God's *daily* grace and forgiveness of our sins. Jesus told Peter that once he had been washed clean, he only needed to wash his feet. In other words, by <u>believing in Christ and accepting Him as our Savior</u>, we are <u>granted eternal life</u>, but we should <u>consider our sins</u> often <u>and confess them to God</u>. Thankfully, His mercies are new every day!

> The Lord's lovingkindnesses indeed never cease, for His compassions never fail. They are new every morning; great is Your faithfulness.
> —Lamentations 3:22–23 NASB

Closing Prayer: Try to close each day's lesson in prayer. You may pray the written prayer aloud if you choose. Father God, help me to fully understand that putting my faith and trust in Your Son, Jesus, washes me clean of my sins and grants me eternal life and fellowship with You. Help me see when I am putting pride and position before You or my service to others. Lord, I want to spend a few moments every day confessing my daily sins and seeking the cleansing that only You can bring. Thank You, Lord, for Your grace, mercy, and love for me. In Jesus' name I pray. Amen.

BLESSED IF YOU DO THEM

Read John 13:12–17 in your Bible.
Next, complete the chart below, verse by verse.

Briefly write what each verse reveals to you about the Father, the Son, or the Holy Spirit. Perhaps the verse reflects a character trait of God (merciful, patient, gentle, loving). The verse might show what the Lord values (obedience, service) or how He wants us to behave (humbly, kindly, compassionately). It's fine to leave some spaces blank since you won't find an answer to the question in every verse. The idea is to read each verse thinking, *Does this verse tell me anything about God?* and then writing what comes to mind.

JOHN 13:12–17	What does this verse tell me about God?
12. When he had washed their feet and put on his outer garments and resumed his place, he said to them, "Do you understand what I have done to you?"	Jesus went from servant to Master, once He finished washing the disciples' feet.
13. "You call me Teacher and Lord, and you are right, for so I am."	Jesus is <u>Lord</u>. Jesus is the <u>Teacher</u>. Jesus is <u>I AM</u>.
14. "If I then, your Lord and Teacher, have washed your feet, you also ought to wash one another's feet."	God values a servant's heart towards others.

What does this verse tell me about God?

15. "For I have given you an example, that you also should do just as I have done to you."	Jesus is our greatest example to learn from. We should follow in His footsteps.
16. "Truly, truly, I say to you, a servant is not greater than his master, nor is a messenger greater than the one who sent him."	Nobody on Earth is greater than the other. We are all equal.
17. "If you know these things, you are blessed if you do them."	God blesses those who have a servant's heart & are humble.

Even at this late hour in Jesus' ministry, most likely a few days before the foot washing, the disciples clearly needed a lesson in humility. Read Luke 22:21–27 and describe the scene:

Jesus said someone will betray him. The disciples argue who was going to betray + who was greater than the other towards Jesus. Jesus interrupts + says "For who is greater the servant or the master? Isn't it the master? But yet, I am here sitting among you, the servants.

The disciples, even though they spent the most time with Jesus, were still focused on things of this world: prestige, position, and pride. Jesus reminded them, "Let the greatest among you become as the youngest, and the leader as one who serves" (v. 26). Jesus also said, "I am among you as the one who serves" (v. 27).

Jesus sent a clear message that not one of them was greater or more important than the others. He pointed out that if He could wash the disciples' feet, they should also serve one another. It is a powerful reminder not to think too much of ourselves.

Think of a time recently when you thought too much of yourself. Write about a time when you allowed your pride or your focus on prestige to shift your focus off Christ.

This past summer, I could of called Kelli, but instead I let it fester because I felt like she wronged me more than I might of offended her.

When Jesus spoke to the disciples after washing their feet, He reminded them of their position with respect to the Lord. The student is not greater than the Teacher and the messenger is not greater than the one who sent him. In other words, we will never be "greater" than our Lord. Also, nothing in our lives should be "greater" than Him.

Next, Jesus gave a clear directive. He gave us an example we should follow (v. 15). As followers of Christ, we are to serve one another without consideration of pride or position. Jesus showed us *how* to serve: with a heart understanding that we are no better or greater than others.

same as "keeping up appearances"

If you are serving because you think you are "supposed to," then you are not serving in love. If you are serving with thoughts that you are so "good" because you volunteer at a local charity, then you are not serving the way Jesus taught us. If you are serving because you feel sorry for someone, you are not serving the way Jesus taught us. Serve because you love the people you are involved with. Consider each and every person, and ask yourself: Do you love them? Is *that* why you are serving?

What activities should you *stop* doing because you are not serving in love?

this is gossip.

- Asking = "How are you" when I'm just trying to get info about the person
- Feeling = bad + helping not because of love but of guilt.
- Thinking = "I want to sing, because I am better than those that have sung a special in church before."

What service could you do with love?

- Sing a special at church w/the intention of loving God, not the attention + praise of man.
- give to the church, not because it's "the right thing to do" or because others tell me I should, but because I want to give back to God's house out of love for the church + it's growth.

Now, let's turn this around. Remember in yesterday's lesson that Peter did not want Jesus to wash his feet. Surely not! But serving one another is what God asked us to do. Are you letting anyone serve you? If not, why aren't you letting anyone help you? Is it pride? Is it fear? Is it selfishness? Turning away help, or not asking for help, is sometimes selfish or prideful. Are you handling something all by yourself so that you alone can take credit? Who are you denying the opportunity to be blessed by serving you? Write your thoughts here:

Teen Group Girl wanted me to join but due to my PRIDE I don't want to be associated w/ her or the group.

Jesus continued His clear message: you will be blessed if you do this. God wants us to use our lives to serve Him by serving others. He assured us that it will not be in vain. Write about the blessings the Lord has provided as a result of serving others. Explain what you have received from doing the work of the Lord.

- After playing w/ little kids (like Lucy) out of the love + kindness of my heart (because I wanted to play w/ them) we got to laugh & connect - which may be a small blessing (being able to laugh, smile, + have fun) but it's still a little fulfilling being respected, wanted, + loved by a little kid.

Be steadfast, immovable, always abounding in the work of the Lord, knowing that in the Lord your labor is not in vain. —1 Corinthians 15:58

Closing Prayer: Father, thank You for being our Teacher and Lord. Thank You for making it so simple to do Your work. I pray that I will serve others with humility and love. Lord, show me the service You would have me do. I want to abound in Your work, Lord. I pray that I will allow the Holy Spirit to guide my way. Thank You for the blessings You give me every day. In Jesus' name I pray. Amen.

WEEK 1 | DAY 3

CHOOSE CHRIST

Read John 13:18–30 in your Bible.
Next, complete the chart below, verse by verse.

Briefly write what each verse reveals to you about the Father, the Son, or the Holy Spirit. Perhaps the verse reflects a character trait of God (merciful, patient, gentle, loving). The verse might show what the Lord values (obedience, service) or how He wants us to behave (humbly, kindly, compassionately). It's fine to leave some spaces blank since you won't find an answer to the question in every verse. The idea is to read each verse thinking, *Does this verse tell me anything about God?* and then writing what comes to mind.

JOHN 13:18–30	What does this verse tell me about God?
18. "I am not speaking of all of you; I know whom I have chosen. But the Scripture will be fulfilled, 'He who ate my bread has lifted his heel against me.'"	
19. "I am telling you this now, before it takes place, that when it does take place you may believe that I am he."	
20. "Truly, truly, I say to you, whoever receives the one I send receives me, and whoever receives me receives the one who sent me."	

What does this verse tell me about God?

21. After saying these things, Jesus was troubled in his spirit, and testified, "Truly, truly, I say to you, one of you will betray me."

22. The disciples looked at one another, uncertain of whom he spoke.

23. One of his disciples, whom Jesus loved, was reclining at table at Jesus' side,

24. so Simon Peter motioned to him to ask Jesus of whom he was speaking.

25. So that disciple, leaning back against Jesus, said to him, "Lord, who is it?"

26. Jesus answered, "It is he to whom I will give this morsel of bread when I have dipped it." So when he had dipped the morsel, he gave it to Judas, the son of Simon Iscariot.

27. Then after he had taken the morsel, Satan entered into him. Jesus said to him, "What you are going to do, do quickly."

28. Now no one at the table knew why he said this to him.

29. Some thought that, because
Judas had the moneybag,
Jesus was telling him, "Buy
what we need for the feast,"
or that he should give
something to the poor.

30. So, after receiving
the morsel of bread, he
immediately went out.
And it was night.

This scene is an example of how God grants understanding in His time. Even though Jesus spoke of the betrayal three times, no one around Him really understood what was going on. Often we cannot understand things when they are happening to us, though we might later. In all things, understanding comes from God.

Write about a time in your life when understanding something that happened to you came later, after the fact:

Verses 19–20 are interesting because Jesus told His disciples that He was telling them things before they happened so they would believe that "I am he." Really? Even the disciples didn't get it. Even the disciples didn't really believe it. These verses tell us that even those closest to Jesus had trouble understanding who Jesus was, or perhaps had their doubts. If you ever stumble or have doubts about God, remember that Jesus understands. Though most Christians will admit they struggle with doubts at times, your faith in Jesus is still the foundation of your relationship with God.

Jesus next became troubled in spirit because of the betrayal, and He told the disciples that one of them would betray Him. They were confused. They could not imagine who among them would betray Jesus. Some said, "Is it I?" (Mark 14:19). The disciples' questions and confusion about the betrayal of Jesus should be a lesson that any of us are capable of grievous sin. If we don't believe this, "we are deluded and have no real idea of how much we owe to the grace of God."[2]

Consider also that Judas was close enough to Jesus that Jesus was able to hand a piece of bread to him (v. 26). Judas *must* have been sitting near enough to hear Jesus say "not all of you are clean" (v. 11) and the reference to Scripture that was to be fulfilled: "He who ate my bread has lifted his heel against me" (v. 18). And again more plainly, "One of you will betray me" (v. 21).

By referencing the betrayal before dipping the bread and handing it to Judas, was Jesus giving Judas a last chance to think again? In their culture, it was considered a gesture of friendship to hand the bread to another during a meal. One commentary put it this way: "No man in history was more 'put on the spot' than Judas in that moment."[3] Judas's acceptance of the bread reflected his choice—his rejection of Christ.

The enemy tempts each of us to sin and we are each capable of giving in. How is the enemy tempting you right now? What choices are you making in your life that reflect the enemy more than they reflect Christ and your faith in Him?

Please understand, as seen in these verses, Jesus gives us endless chances to choose His way and reject Satan's prompting. Next time, in that moment when you must choose, picture Jesus sitting next to you holding out a piece of bread and giving you a chance to choose His way, a chance to make the right choice. Take each thing you wrote above and write how you could choose differently. Make it some sort of action, not just a thought or emotion. What could you do at that moment when you must choose?

Let's look at what happened when Judas made his choice. Jesus commanded Judas to "do quickly" what he was about to do. Although prompted by Satan, Jesus was still in control of Judas and the situation. Jesus was not a victim of His circumstances. He went willingly to the cross . . . for you. Why? Because He loves you infinitely more than you can imagine *and* because Jesus desired to do the will of the Father:

> From that time Jesus began to show his disciples that he must go to Jerusalem and suffer many things from the elders and chief priests and scribes, and be killed, and on the third day be raised. And Peter took him aside and began to rebuke him, saying, "Far be it from you, Lord! This shall never happen to you." But he turned and said to Peter, "Get behind me, Satan! You are a hindrance to me. For you are not setting your mind on the things of God, but on the things of man." (Matthew 16:21–23)

Perhaps when you feel tempted and before you take the actions you listed above, you could say, "Get behind me, Satan! You will not be a stumbling block to me. I will keep my mind on God's interests, not my own!"

Take comfort, however, in the fact that even when you do not stand firm and make the right choice, Jesus is still in control. Jesus still commands you and your life.

> "For I know the plans I have for you," declares the LORD, "plans to prosper you and not to harm you, plans to give you hope and a future."
> —Jeremiah 29:11 NIV

Closing Prayer: Father, I am overwhelmed by Your love for me. I am overwhelmed by Your humility in letting me choose You, even when You command all things. Thank You, Lord, for loving me so much that You would give me so many chances to choose Your way. Lord, help me stop and consider You in the daily choices in my life. Help me make the choices that would be pleasing to You. Thank You for loving me enough to make plans for me in Your kingdom. In Jesus' name I pray. Amen.

WEEK 1 | DAY 4

THE NEW COMMANDMENT

Read John 13:31–38 in your Bible.
Next, complete the chart below, verse by verse.

Briefly write what each verse reveals to you about the Father, the Son, or the Holy Spirit. Perhaps the verse reflects a character trait of God (merciful, patient, gentle, loving). The verse might show what the Lord values (obedience, service) or how He wants us to behave (humbly, kindly, compassionately). It's fine to leave some spaces blank since you won't find an answer to the question in every verse. The idea is to read each verse thinking, *Does this verse tell me anything about God?* and then writing what comes to mind.

JOHN 13:31–38	What does this verse tell me about God?
31. When he had gone out, Jesus said, "Now is the Son of Man glorified, and God is glorified in Him."	
32. "If God is glorified in him, God will also glorify him in himself, and glorify him at once."	
33. "Little children, yet a little while I am with you. You will seek me, and just as I said to the Jews, so now I also say to you, 'Where I am going you cannot come.'"	

34. "A new commandment I give to you, that you love one another: just as I have loved you, you also are to love one another."

35. "By this all people will know that you are my disciples, if you have love for one another."

36. Simon Peter said to him, "Lord, where are you going?" Jesus answered him, "Where I am going you cannot follow me now, but you will follow afterward."

37. Peter said to him, "Lord, why can I not follow you now? I will lay down my life for you."

38. Jesus answered, "Will you lay down your life for me? Truly, truly, I say to you, the rooster will not crow till you have denied me three times."

Jesus told us that God would be glorified through the Son of Man. How? One commentator put it this way: "Had God remained aloof and majestic, serene and unmoved, untouched by any sorrow, unhurt by any pain, men might have feared Him and men might have admired Him; but they would never have loved Him."[4]

Take a moment to reflect on all that Jesus sacrificed to lower Himself to become a man on earth, die on the cross, and bear all of your sins. Consider whether your life is honoring His great love for you. Write about any changes the Holy Spirit reveals to you about your life or choices:

Next, Jesus told the disciples that He would be with them only a little while longer. But notice that He called them "little children." Jesus probably was speaking to the disciples in this way so they could understand and appreciate their new relationship with the Father. As believers in Christ, we belong to the Father. We are children of God.

Jesus gave His followers a new commandment. In the New International Version it is stated this way: "A new command I give you: Love one another. As I have loved you, so you must love one another. By this everyone will know that you are my disciples, if you love one another" (vv. 34–35). What does this verse mean to you?

Our love for one another is a shining light to lead others to Christ. It is a call to live by *His* mission: to serve one another in love, with a self-sacrificing love for each other. It is a call to grant forgiveness to others. It is a call to humble ourselves, a call to stand out in the crowd. It is a call to keep our priorities straight, and lead by example. It is a call to spread the good news of the gospel.

Read Colossians 3:12–14. List what we are to "put on" as people who have been chosen by God:

Write some things you could do to "love one another as I have loved you" or how you could "put on love" this week. Be as specific as possible.

We are not Jesus, so we cannot, unfortunately, be perfect. If we ignore our imperfections and forget to confess our sins, we are not truly living in God's grace. So write down when you were not a shining light this week that would lead others to Christ.

Call on Jesus and ask Him to forgive you. Ask that the Holy Spirit guide your every word, every act, and every thought as you go through your day.

Let's continue to look at God's promise in our passage today. Peter asked where the Lord was going and Jesus responded, "Where I am going you cannot follow me now, but you will follow afterward." Take notice that there was no "maybe." Jesus was firm. You *will* follow later.

Peter did not want to wait until later (don't you love him!). He told Jesus, "I will lay down my life for you." Jesus responded, "Will you lay down your life for me?"

What if Jesus asked you that question? When push comes to shove, would you lay down your life for Jesus? Really? Let's start small. What are you currently giving up to serve Him? What are you already laying down to follow Jesus?

Instead of laying down his life for Jesus, Peter betrayed Him. Jesus knew of Peter's betrayal and told him about it before it happened as we're told in verse 38. What was the point of this prediction? Write your thoughts here:

What if this verse is meant to encourage us? Perhaps this Scripture is meant to give us hope. If Peter, one of Jesus' most loyal followers and a leader among the disciples, could deny Him when times got tough, we are all capable of denying Christ. Yet, the Lord is incredibly patient and loving toward us. We should not have confidence in ourselves, but in Christ alone.

We should also consider prayer as a powerful weapon against the enemy. Jesus gave us a great example with regard to Peter:

> "Simon, Simon, behold, Satan demanded to have you, that he might sift you like wheat, but I have prayed for you that your faith may not fail. And when you have turned again, strengthen your brothers."
> —Luke 22:31–32

Jesus prayed for His disciples. Even His disciples needed prayers for protection, and if they needed such prayers, you can be certain that we do too! Thankfully, we are not alone, even when we do not know just how to pray, and even in those times when we can barely form words. We're told in Romans 8:26–27, "Likewise the Spirit helps us in our weakness. For we do not know what to pray for as we ought, but the Spirit himself intercedes for us with groanings too deep for words. And he who searches hearts knows what is the mind of the Spirit, because the Spirit intercedes for the saints according to the will of God."

How comforting to know that the Spirit of God "intercedes for us with groanings too deep for words." I don't know about you, but that brings great comfort to me, knowing that He was interceding for me when I lost Austin. We're also told in Romans 8:34 that "Christ Jesus who is at the right hand of God is interceding for us."

Have there been times in your own life when your pain or sorrow was so deep that you couldn't even find the words to pray? Write your thoughts here.

What does it mean to you right now in your own journey that the Spirit intercedes for you?

"With everlasting love I will have compassion on you," says the LORD your Redeemer. —Isaiah 54:8

Closing Prayer: Lord, Your lovingkindness humbles me. Thank You for being patient with my weaknesses and forgiving of my failures. Help me love others as You love me. Father, I want to show Your light to everyone around me. I want others to know that I follow You because of the way I behave toward my family, friends, neighbors, and community. I want to have the strength, courage, and faith to lay down the things of this world to serve You, Lord. Thank You for interceding for me. Make me a prayer warrior for others. In Jesus' name I pray. Amen.

REVIEW, REFLECT, AND PRAY

Before you begin today, ask God to reveal anything you may
have missed the first time through the lessons. Take time to review
the verses for each day and fill in any spaces you left blank, if you
can. Remember that only God through the Holy Spirit grants
understanding, especially when it comes to God's Word. And be
assured it's okay if you have empty spaces.

Read what you wrote about God in each chart and write your
thoughts here:

Next, review what you wrote in response to the questions in each lesson and take a
few minutes to pray about what God wants you to learn.

If God revealed something to you this week, note it here:

If God reminded you of something you have been forgetting lately, or if the Holy
Spirit showed you something that has not been part of your life for a while, write
about it here:

If God challenged you to make a change in your life, how did He do it and what change will you make?

Before you end this week, take a few moments to be quiet and still. Take time to let the lessons become wisdom in your heart. Be still and let the Lord speak into your heart about what service you should do to "love one another."

"Be still, and know that I am God." —Psalm 46:10 NIV

Closing Prayer: Father God, this time with You is so precious. Thank You for Your Word and Your everlasting lovingkindness. I want to be transformed in Christ's image. I know that only Your grace can make me more like Jesus. Father, help me love others as You have loved me. Guide me to the service of others that You would have me do. In the name of my Lord Jesus I pray. Amen.

In John 13, we read that Jesus washed the apostles' feet and told them plainly that He gave them an example to follow. Jesus explained that we will be blessed if we humbly serve others. The pattern of obedience followed by blessing is repeated over and over again in the Bible. Jesus promised such blessings in the New Testament, and the Old Testament is filled with examples of God's people being blessed after they obeyed God. So why is it so difficult? Why do we struggle to humble ourselves and serve others? Why do we find it so hard to love one another as ourselves?

I wonder if it has to do with an inflated sense of self. We seem to be wired with a constant refrain of "hey, what about me?" People are inherently worried about whether they are getting what others are getting. One day at the store, I picked up some gum at the checkout counter and my six-year-old son immediately said, "Hey, what about me? Do I get to pick something too?" Think about how often you compare what you have to what someone else has. I can't recall many times in my life where I honestly thought, "Boy, I am so glad that she has _____ and I don't." Perhaps we are so overtaken by the "what about me" thinking that we fill our lives with activities that are supposed to help us get more of what we think other people seem to have. Our lives revolve around getting more happiness, contentment, security, money, time, pleasure, and so on.[5] What if we could change our "what about me?" into "what about others?" What would our lives look like if we could consistently be motivated by "what about others?"

During this week's lessons, we explored *why* the Lord wants us to serve others and love one another. "By this all people will know that you are my disciples, if you have love for one another" (John 13:35). Jesus did not mention anything about serving others because others need our help. He did not tell us to serve others so that we can receive blessings (hey, what about me?). Jesus told us to serve others so others will know about Him. Loving one another is about pointing others to Jesus!

He did tell us that we *will* be blessed if we do these things, but the blessing is not the reason Jesus commanded us to love one another. We must do so because we are motivated by His great love and we want to share that love with the world. We must serve others with a heart that is focused on showing people the love of Christ.

If people can feel the love of Christ wash over them as we serve them, they will wonder what we have that they don't. Let the door open for us to share the gospel, because what we have that they don't is Christ. If we can simply love one another, then others will be directed to Christ.

So as you continue this study and begin to think of ways to serve others, think of how you could serve in love *only*. Do not consider who "needs" you. Do not consider what you can do well. Do not consider what others will recognize or value. You should *only* consider what you might be able to do in complete and total love.

Write your ideas here:

We will circle back to this challenge at the end of our study. I can't wait to hear how God uses you to lead others to Him!

LOVE ONE ANOTHER

1. Review the lessons and what you wrote for Day 5. Share insights with the group.

2. Jesus washed Judas's feet, knowing this apostle would betray Him. Is there someone that you need to show love and compassion toward, even though it's especially difficult? Maybe others in the group could help you think of a way to "wash the feet" of that person.

3. Tell the group about a blessing you received, or are still receiving, from serving others.

4. Read Matthew 16:21–23 out loud. Can you identify where you do not "have in mind the concerns of God, but merely human concerns"? (NIV) When this comes up the next time, pray quickly, "Get behind me, Satan!" and remind yourself that the things of God are most important. Consider putting a note that says, "Get behind me, Satan!" or "GBMS!" near the place where this most often happens to you during the day.

5. If it would encourage the group, share one thing you did to love one another this week.

6. Gather prayer requests for the week and close in prayer.

Jesus is the way, the truth, and the life

JOHN 14

Before I became a true believer in Christ, I used to think people who said that their way was the only way to get to heaven were narrow-minded, uneducated, or judgmental.

I thought folks who said Jesus was the *only* way to heaven had no right to say whether or not I would go there. Since I did not know much about the Bible, I believed these people were just sharing their own opinions. I did not consider the Bible to be the Word of God, but thought of it as a dusty book that old guys wrote thousands of years ago, writings that couldn't possibly have anything to do with me.

Shortly after I gave my life to Jesus Christ, my pastor was sitting at our kitchen table discussing the fact that when you truly make Jesus your Lord and Savior, you receive the gift of the Holy Spirit. I was waiting for lightning to strike him down! Seriously, I gaped at him with an open mouth and wide eyes. When I was young, my family went to church and I heard all about the Father, Son, and Holy Spirit. Unfortunately, I completely missed the point. The Holy Spirit, I thought, was the power of God that made things happen in the universe. You didn't dare think that you, a lowly human, could have anything to do with the Holy Spirit. You wouldn't dare claim that you had the power of God. I thought surely my pastor was about to bring that power of God down on my kitchen!

Next, my pastor explained that the Holy Spirit helps a believer read and understand the Bible. Since lightning hadn't struck him down and he was still there talking, I was listening, but now I was frowning. *Hmmm . . . really?* The Bible had never made much sense to me, so I usually put it down after trying to read a brief passage. I was wondering if my pastor was right about this Holy Spirit thing. It might explain why some people were so passionate about the Bible and others just didn't get it.

I could test what my pastor said. I decided to start reading my brand-new Bible, but I did so with a skeptical mind.

Since I am the author of this study, you might be able to guess what happened when I started reading! The Holy Spirit did a powerful work in me through the Word of God. Over and over again, as I began reading the New Testament, I felt that He was speaking directly to me. Not only did I understand what I read, but I felt a deep stirring in my heart of things that had previously been hidden. I felt that secrets of the world were explained right there in the Bible.

> **When was the last time you were overwhelmed by the power of the Holy Spirit? When was the last time you read your Bible in utter astonishment?**

Often when I had a specific worry or hurt, the Holy Spirit would lead me to read something that helped me. Sometimes I would stop and look around. I thought I needed a "reality check"—was this really happening to me? I had to see if anyone was watching me read my Bible and saw the tears running down my face or my mouth open in amazement or my head bowed in humility.

I was overwhelmed by the Holy Spirit and the Bible. Through the Bible, the Holy Spirit showed me the love of God. As I read, I began to truly understand the heart of the Creator of the universe. Such understanding, my friends, is the power of God through the power of the Holy Spirit. The Holy Spirit is within you as a believer in Jesus as the way, the truth, and the life!

If you grew up knowing these truths, these concepts might seem basic to you. But I wonder, when was the last time you were overwhelmed by the power of the Holy Spirit? When was the last time you read your Bible in utter astonishment? When was the last time you practically jumped up and down because the Lord of the universe just spoke to you through the Word? If you know and understand these truths, do you call on the power of the Holy Spirit throughout your day, every single day? If this is "old hat" to you, my prayer is that this week's lessons will give you a new revelation that only the Spirit, our Teacher, could give you to deepen your understanding and passion for Christ and God's Word.

This week, you will read about how Jesus and the Father are one. You will read that Jesus promised to send His followers the Holy Spirit, who would teach them all things. It is one of the most amazing promises in the Bible because He provides the way, the truth, and the life through Christ. The Holy Spirit is the power of Christ in us. The gift of the Holy Spirit is what makes a relationship with God possible. Our reliance on the power of the Holy Spirit is the only way we can hope to lead a life that is pleasing to our Lord. John 14 explains why lightning will not strike you down when you claim the power of the Holy Spirit in your life. Instead, Jesus promises that the Holy Spirit will be with you and guide your way.

Prepare yourself for a powerful week. Take extra time with the lessons and let the Holy Spirit reveal or refresh these wonderful mysteries in your soul.

WEEK 2 | DAY 1

NO ONE COMES TO THE FATHER BUT THROUGH ME

Read John 14:1–6 in your Bible.
Then complete the chart below.

Briefly write what each verse reveals to you about the Father, the Son, or the Holy Spirit. Perhaps the verse reflects a character trait of God (merciful, patient, gentle, loving). The verse might show what the Lord values (obedience, service) or how He wants us to behave (humbly, kindly, compassionately). It's fine to leave some spaces blank since you won't find an answer to the question in every verse. The idea is to read each verse thinking, *Does this verse tell me anything about God?* and then writing what comes to mind.

JOHN 14:1–6	What does this verse tell me about God?
1. "Let not your hearts be troubled. Believe in God; believe also in me."	
2. "In my Father's house are many rooms. If it were not so, would I have told you that I go to prepare a place for you?"	
3. "And if I go and prepare a place for you, I will come again and will take you to myself, that where I am you may be also."	

4. "And you know the way to where I am going."

5. Thomas said to him, "Lord, we do not know where you are going. How can we know the way?"

6. Jesus said to him, "I am the way, and the truth, and the life. No one comes to the Father except through me."

Jesus just finished telling Peter that he would betray Jesus three times before the rooster crowed, and His next words to His friends were "let not your hearts be troubled. Believe in God; believe also in me."

Jesus was preparing His disciples for what would come next: the scattering of the disciples, His crucifixion, and His death. Yet, He simply told His disciples to believe in Him. Belief in Him and belief in God is meant to comfort us. If we believe in God and in Jesus His Son, how can our hearts remain troubled for very long? If we believe in God and that Jesus is His Son, then we believe in an eternal life that is in fellowship with the Father and the Son. What, then, could be so important during our brief stay here that we allow our hearts to remain troubled for very long?

What is troubling you today? What are your struggles, difficulties, or worries?

Pray over what you wrote, perhaps something like this: *Father, I believe in You and I believe in Jesus Your Son. I look forward to the time when I will live with You in an eternal life of fellowship and worship of You. Please help me remain focused on You and not on the troubles of this world. Lord, please help me release what is troubling my heart, and rest in my belief in You and Your love for me.*

After being comforted by Jesus, the disciples next heard a promise. Many dwelling places are in His Father's house and Jesus was going to prepare a place for them. This promise should give us amazing hope and peace. Jesus has prepared a place for you! But don't stop there—read on. It only makes sense that if He prepared a place for you, He will come for you and bring you to that place.

How do you react to this promise? What does this promise tell us about the character of God?

John 12:26 says, "If anyone serves me, he must follow me; and where I am, there will my servant be also. If anyone serves me, the Father will honor him." Jesus promised several times during His time with the disciples that believers would join Him in heaven.

Next, it is key that Jesus did not say the disciples would know where He was going, but rather know "the way" to get where He was going . . . meaning they knew how to get there. In fact, Thomas pointed out, "We do not know where you are going. How can we know the way?" (John 14:5)

Jesus responded, "I am the way, and the truth, and the life. No one comes to the Father except through me."

Initially, we want to cheer at this statement. YES! Jesus *is* the way, the truth, and the life! In John 6:47, Jesus said plainly, "Truly, truly, I say to you, whoever believes has eternal life." Jesus later added, "I am the door. If anyone enters by me, he will be saved and will go in and out and find pasture" (John 10:9).

But then Jesus reminded us that not everyone will have eternal life with the Father. "No one comes to the Father except through me." What a difficult thing to hear and believe. Some people will spend eternity in heaven and some will not. First John 5:20 tell us, "And we know that the Son of God has come and has given us understanding, so that we may know him who is true; and we are in him who is true, in his Son Jesus Christ. He is the true God and eternal life." Faith in Christ is the way to eternal life. It's that simple.

Read John 11:20–27 about when Martha goes out to meet Jesus after Lazarus died.

1. What was Jesus' statement to Martha?

2. What did Jesus ask her?

3. What was Martha's response?

Do you truly believe? Do you have people close to you who do not believe in Jesus? Please remember that Jesus also explained, "No one can come to me unless the Father who sent me draws him" (John 6:44). As we encounter and pray for those who do not yet believe in Christ as their Savior, we need to remember that God must first call someone. Only God can turn the hearts of people. It is He who must first draw people to Jesus. Only the Father can call His children to Him.

Write the names of three people you know who do not know Jesus as their Savior. Pray for each one that the Father would open their hearts and call him or her, that He would cause them to seek Jesus. Ask the Father for opportunities to share the truth with these individuals.

To me, these verses mean that although we had to choose to believe in Jesus as our Savior, first the Father had to choose us. Doesn't that just blow you away? He wants you as His beloved. He thinks you are precious. Can you just be still for a moment and let this sink in?

If you let the fact that God chose to die for *you* become wisdom within you, it can serve as an anchor for your life. When you run into trouble, when you encounter difficulties, when you experience self-doubt, you can sit back and rest in the knowledge that God chose to die for you. A Christian song includes these words: "This one's Mine." I love that part of the song. Can you imagine hearing God say it out loud . . . "this one is Mine" . . . and He means *you*?

But you still have to ask for His grace. You have to accept that He has chosen you and receive the gift of salvation. In Matthew 7:7–8, Jesus said, "Ask, and it will be given to you; seek, and you will find; knock, and it will be opened to you. For everyone who asks receives, and the one who seeks finds, and to the one who knocks it will be opened."

Here is a reminder that we must believe that Jesus rewards those who seek Him:

> And without faith it is impossible to please him, for whoever would draw near to God must believe that he exists and that he rewards those who seek him. —Hebrews 11:6

Closing Prayer: Father, thank You for comforting me and loving me. I am humbled that You would prepare a place for me and allow me to spend eternity with You. Lord, thank You for choosing me and showing me the way, the truth, and the life. Without You, I would be lost. I am so grateful for the promise that someday I will be with You forever. I want Jesus to be the Lord of my life. I give it all to You, Jesus. In Jesus' name I pray. Amen.

WEEK 2 | DAY 2

I AM IN THE FATHER
AND THE FATHER IS IN ME

Read John 14:7–15 in your Bible.
Then complete the chart below.

Briefly write what each verse reveals to you about the Father, the Son, or the Holy Spirit. Perhaps the verse reflects a character trait of God (merciful, patient, gentle, loving). The verse might show what the Lord values (obedience, service) or how He wants us to behave (humbly, kindly, compassionately). It's fine to leave some spaces blank since you won't find an answer to the question in every verse. The idea is to read each verse thinking, *Does this verse tell me anything about God?* and then writing what comes to mind.

JOHN 14:7–15	What does this verse tell me about God?
7. "If you had known me, you would have known my Father also. From now on you do know him and have seen him."	
8. Philip said to him, "Lord, show us the Father, and it is enough for us."	
9. Jesus said to him, "Have I been with you so long, and you still do not know me, Philip? Whoever has seen me has seen the Father. How can you say, 'Show us the Father'?"	

What does this verse tell me about God?

10. "Do you not believe that I am in the Father, and the Father is in me? The words that I say to you I do not speak on my own authority, but the Father who dwells in me does his works."

11. "Believe me that I am in the Father and the Father is in me, or else believe on account of the works themselves."

12. "Truly, truly, I say to you, whoever believes in me will also do the works that I do; and greater works than these will he do, because I am going to the Father."

13. "Whatever you ask in my name, this will I do, that the Father may be glorified in the Son."

14. "If you ask me anything in my name, I will do it."

15. "If you love me, you will keep my commandments."

From now on, you know the Father. No wonder Philip didn't really get it. Can't you relate to Philip? Just show us the Father. I can just picture him looking around the room . . . where? Show us and it will be enough! Though Philip and the others didn't completely understand at that time, Paul later bluntly put the truth Jesus was explaining like this: "In Christ all the fullness of the Deity lives in bodily form" (Colossians 2:9 NIV).

Then Jesus responded by asking whether Philip believed Him. Jesus explained again that the Father was working through Him. Then Jesus continued . . . and if you don't believe that, then believe because of the works themselves. At the very least, if you must, look at the miracles Jesus performed and believe He is from God because of those miracles. But notice that first He asked Philip to believe Him because Philip knew Jesus. Jesus wants us to believe in Him by faith, because we know Him and believe Him. That would be His first choice—that we simply believe He is our Savior from the Father.

Write three miracles Jesus performed that help you believe that Jesus was from the Father and performing the works of the Father:

Jesus next said something that can be difficult to understand: "Whoever believes in me will also do the works that I do; and greater works than these will he do, because I am going to the Father" (v. 12). Though some believe Jesus is saying His followers will do miraculous things on earth, He is really telling them that, though He was confined geographically to a certain area during His time on earth, future disciples will spread the gospel throughout the whole world. These are the "greater works."

Take another look at this verse and write how you can do "greater works":

The last part of our passage today is often used by folks who feel they have been let down by God as an excuse to be angry with Him. Verse 14 says, "If you ask me anything in my name, I will do it." We must, however, read the verses surrounding this promise. First, the request must glorify God through the Son (v. 13). Second, Jesus reminded us that if we love Him, we will keep His commandments (v. 15). These three verses combined tell us that if we are walking with God, seeking to glorify Him, and praying for things that are His will, He will respond to our prayers. It does not say that we will get whatever we want. It does not say that if we pray for something and then at the end tack on, "in Jesus' name, Amen" that our prayers will be answered as we demand.

Are there things you have prayed about, but did not receive? Did you feel a bit entitled to get what you asked for because you thought it would serve God? Write those matters here and release them to God's will. Pray that the Holy Spirit will help you be content without the fulfillment of those prayers and grateful for the many blessings you have received.

John later wrote, "And this is love, that we walk according to his commandments" (2 John 6). He was speaking of the commandment to walk in truth and to love one another. Look back at Week 1, Day 4 and pray about the things you identified as ways you could "love one another." How are you doing with those ideas? Write about your progress (or lack thereof) here and ask for God to help you shine His light on others.

But you are a chosen race, a royal priesthood, a holy nation, a people for his own possession, that you may proclaim the excellencies of him who called you out of darkness into his marvelous light. —1 Peter 2:9

Closing Prayer: Lord, thank You for forgiving our unbelief and for being patient with us while we struggle to comprehend Your majesty and power. Father, I believe in You and in Jesus Christ Your Son. I believe that You are in Him and He is in You. I am humbled and in awe that, because of my faith, I am also in You and You are in me. I pray that I will use Your dwelling in me through the Holy Spirit to keep Your commandment to love one another. In Jesus' name I pray. Amen.

WEEK 2 | DAY 3

THE HOLY SPIRIT

Read John 14:16–24 in your Bible.
Next, complete the chart below, verse by verse.

Briefly write what each verse reveals to you about the Father, the Son, or the Holy Spirit. Perhaps the verse reflects a character trait of God (merciful, patient, gentle, loving). The verse might show what the Lord values (obedience, service) or how He wants us to behave (humbly, kindly, compassionately). It's fine to leave some spaces blank since you won't find an answer to the question in every verse. The idea is to read each verse thinking, *Does this verse tell me anything about God?* and then writing what comes to mind.

JOHN 14:16–24	What does this verse tell me about God?
16. "I will ask the Father, and he will give you another Helper, to be with you forever,"	
17. "even the Spirit of truth, whom the world cannot receive, because it neither sees him nor knows him. You know him, for he dwells with you and will be in you."	
18. "I will not leave you as orphans; I will come to you."	

What does this verse tell me about God?

19. "Yet a little while and the world will see me no more, but you will see me. Because I live, you also will live."

20. "In that day you will know that I am in my Father, and you in me, and I in you."

21. "Whoever has my commandments and keeps them, he it is who loves me. And he who loves me will be loved by my Father, and I will love him and manifest myself to him."

22. Judas (not Iscariot) said to him, "Lord, how is it that you will manifest yourself to us, and not to the world?"

23. Jesus answered him, "If anyone loves me, he will keep my word, and my Father will love him, and we will come to him and make our home with him."

24. "Whoever does not love me does not keep my words. And the word that you hear is not mine but the Father's who sent me."

The Holy Spirit has been called, among other titles, the Comforter, Advocate, and Intercessor. Jesus and the Holy Spirit also are described as the source of living water in several places throughout the Bible. For example, in John 7:37–39, Jesus said, "If anyone thirsts, let him come to me and drink. Whoever believes in me, as the Scripture has said, 'Out of his heart will flow rivers of living water.' Now this he said about the Spirit, whom those who believed in him were to receive, for as yet the Spirit had not been given, because Jesus was not yet glorified." John later wrote, "And he said to me, 'It is done! I am the Alpha and the Omega, the beginning and the end. To the thirsty I will give from the spring of the water of life without payment'" (Revelation 21:6).

So many important truths are contained in just this passage from Revelation that we could do a whole study on it! It is done. The debt for our sin has been paid. Jesus is *it*! The beginning and the end. He will give to those who seek Him the water of life . . . without cost. Salvation is from Jesus alone and it is by grace alone . . . without cost. Thirst for Him, and He will give you the water of life . . . eternal life with Him. Eternal life begins as soon as we receive Him, i.e., eternal life is not *only* heaven after death (a wondrous truth itself!), but eternal life is also the joyful life we can live with Him during our time on earth. Spend a moment praising God for His amazing lovingkindness.

Read Romans 8:26 and describe a time in your life that fits what is described here:

Now read John 14:17 again. Nonbelievers do not get help from the Holy Spirit, but you do! First Corinthians 2:14 explains, "The natural person does not accept the things of the Spirit of God, for they are folly to him, and he is not able to understand them because they are spiritually discerned." Do you ever feel that the

Holy Spirit, your Helper, is moving in you like living water? Or maybe you sense that small, still voice leading you or putting something on your heart or mind? If you shared your experience with the Holy Spirit with others, pre-believers may have made you feel like what you experienced was foolishness or crazy.

I remember when I was a new believer and this happened to me over and over again as I began to spend time in prayer and study of God's Word. I was overwhelmed by how often the Holy Spirit would reveal something to me. It was amazing, but I was reluctant to share it with many of my friends because, from the world's perspective, it might seem a little crazy. My journey with God began after we lost our son Austin, and I thought folks would think I was hearing voices . . . how sad that they did not understand the truth.

Please let me encourage you to call on the Holy Spirit and do not discount that small, still voice in your heart. The Holy Spirit is real, and He is one of God's most treasured and powerful promises.

Write about a memorable moment when you knew the Holy Spirit was leading, speaking, comforting. Don't feel foolish. Feel chosen and special. Feel blessed to experience moments with the Helper.

Throughout this chapter, Jesus described the Trinity, telling His disciples that He is from the Father, that the words He speaks and the works He performs are from the Father. Jesus explained that He is in the Father and the Father is in Him. But be careful that you do not miss the rest. Jesus told us that He would not leave us as orphans, that He would come to us, that we would be in Him and He in us (vv.18–20)! Our faith in Jesus makes us one with Him and the Father. Verse 21 goes on to explain that whoever loves Jesus will be loved by the Father.

Take a moment and write about a time when you knew you are loved by the Father:

In verses 21 and 23, Jesus told the disciples again that if they loved Him, they would keep His commands, keep His word. He reminded them in verse 24 that His word is not His, but the Father's. You might be thinking that keeping His commandments means that you have to earn your relationship with the Father, but look closer. Once you declare that Jesus is the way, the truth, and the life—accepting His sacrifice for your sins—you will receive the Holy Spirit. God will dwell in you and you will dwell with God! Never again will you struggle alone against sin. Never again will you be alone in making decisions. Call on the power of God who lives within you.

Also, note that the command He referenced twice in the context of "keep my commands" is to "love one another as I have loved you." The commandment is not the same as saying, "sin no more." In fact, Webster's Dictionary defines "to keep" as: "to continue having or holding (something): to not return, lose, sell, give away, or throw away (something); to continue in a specified state, condition, or position; to cause (someone or something) to continue in a specified state, condition, or position."[6]

Jesus meant that if we love Him, we will care about His commands and desire that His commands persevere through our lives.

Describe a few things you could do in your daily life to keep His commandments as a focus in your life:

Another thing we should not miss in today's passage is that Judas (not Iscariot; this Judas is also called Thaddaeus, as in Mark 3:18) asked Jesus why He would disclose Himself to the disciples, but not to the world. Jesus responded by stating (again) that those who love Him will keep His Word and that the Father will love them *and* that they "will come to him and make our home with him" (v. 23). "We," the Father and the Son, will come to you. To me, this spoke again of the Father's choice. "We will come." What a wonderful truth that our God comes to us! If you choose Jesus, our God will abide in you. Such a promise is almost too much to comprehend, isn't it?

> For we are the temple of the living God; as God said, "I will make my dwelling among them and walk among them, and I will be their God, and they shall be my people." —2 Corinthians 6:16

Closing Prayer: Father, thank You for choosing me and loving me. I pray that I will comprehend the power of the Holy Spirit that is within me. Lord, help me comprehend that You dwell in me through the Holy Spirit. I pray for Your divine Spirit to guide my daily life so that each day my focus is to keep Your Word. I want to live a life that sets me apart as Your chosen one. Father, I love You, and it is my heart's desire to follow Christ and keep Your commandments. In Jesus' name I pray. Amen.

WEEK 2 | DAY 4

THE HOLY SPIRIT WILL TEACH
YOU ALL THINGS

Read John 14:25–31 in your Bible.
Next, complete the chart below, verse by verse.

Briefly write what each verse reveals to you about the Father, the Son, or the Holy Spirit. Perhaps the verse reflects a character trait of God (merciful, patient, gentle, loving). The verse might show what the Lord values (obedience, service) or how He wants us to behave (humbly, kindly, compassionately). It's fine to leave some spaces blank since you won't find an answer to the question in every verse. The idea is to read each verse thinking, *Does this verse tell me anything about God?* and then writing what comes to mind.

JOHN 14:25–31	**What does this verse tell me about God?**
25. "These things I have spoken to you while I am still with you."	
26. "But the Helper, the Holy Spirit, whom the Father will send in my name, he will teach you all things and bring to your remembrance all that I have said to you."	
27. "Peace I leave with you; my peace I give to you. Not as the world gives do I give to you. Let not your hearts be troubled, neither let them be afraid."	

What does this verse tell me about God?

28. "You heard me say to you, 'I am going away, and I will come to you.' If you loved me, you would have rejoiced because I am going to the Father, for the Father is greater than I."

29. "And now I have told you before it takes place, so that when it does take place you may believe."

30. "I will no longer talk much with you, for the ruler of this world is coming. He has no claim on me,"

31. "but I do as the Father has commanded me, so that the world may know that I love the Father. Rise, let us go from here."

What a promise! The Holy Spirit will teach you all things. How often in your daily life do you call on the Holy Spirit? John wrote,

> But the anointing that you received from him abides in you, and you have no need that anyone should teach you. But as his anointing teaches you about everything, and is true, and is no lie—just as it has taught you, abide in him. —1 John 2:27

Did you catch that last part? The Holy Spirit will teach you all things. Can you comprehend what that means? Because of your faith in Christ, you have the help of the Holy Spirit. You have a direct relationship with God. Let me say it another way: you are a child of God who has the gift of the Holy Spirit. What power, wisdom, or comfort could this bring to your life?

Write below or journal about something that you feel powerless to change. Write about something for which you need God's divine wisdom and guidance. Or, write about any areas of your life where you need God's peace.

Next, pull out your calendar and set a time every day, perhaps in the morning, to ask God to help you with what you wrote. Set aside time every day, even if it is just ten minutes, to let the Holy Spirit guide you and help you. Be still so you don't miss His voice within you. Be patient. He may not answer right away! But you will know His voice. As Jesus described Himself as our shepherd, He said, "The sheep hear his voice, and he calls his own sheep by name and leads them out. When he has brought out all his own, he goes before them, and the sheep follow him, for they know his voice" (John 10:3–4).

If the things you wrote above are major life decisions or changes, consider allowing at least forty days of seeking God's will before you make a decision. God often used forty days to prepare His people. In fact, even the temptation of Jesus lasted forty days. If you have a major decision to make, write down the date that is forty days from today: _____.

Make a commitment to seek God's will for the next forty days and commit to the process. Make a commitment that you will not make a decision until this date has passed. Even if you think the Lord has been clear, waiting to finish the forty days usually will not be a problem. Forty days to consider and pray about a major life decision is not long in the span of your life. Use the time to listen for God's will to guide you through the Holy Spirit. Use the time to listen for His voice.

What if what you wrote above is not a major life decision, but rather an ongoing and recurring problem that you struggle with every day? Perhaps you wrote about eating healthy, or losing your temper, or keeping your priorities focused on God. For me, it is all of the above! Right now, I am focused on eating healthy. I struggle to avoid junk food and fast food, which I crave. I used to put pictures of "skinny" me on the refrigerator or put my skinny jeans in the front of my closet where I would easily see them. I used to berate myself for not having any self-discipline.

Once I began to know the Lord, I used to pray for more self-discipline, but I would still fail and feel terrible that I did not seem to care enough about God or my body to resist junk food. I felt sincerely worthless because I could not control myself. Do you read all of the "I" and "my" words here?

As I grew in my faith and study of God's Word, He blessed me with a new level of spiritual maturity. I began to understand that the power of the Holy Spirit dwells within me. I can do anything with His help! I realized that I had been trying to take on this problem myself, without God's help, when in reality, I could do nothing apart from Him. My prayers changed and my focus changed. Now I pray for the Holy Spirit (not me) to direct my eating and exercise habits. I pray that I will seek and hear the Holy Spirit's wisdom and guidance for living a healthy lifestyle.

For the daily struggles, are you trying to fix them yourself? Are you calling on God to help you with what may seem like minor things in your life that you think you should be able to tackle yourself? After all, let's leave God to handle all the "big" problems in this world, right? Wrong. The Holy Spirit dwells within us for a reason. He is our Helper for a reason. The Holy Spirit is the Father's gift to you when you put your faith in Jesus alone for eternal life with God. You should not only receive Him but be mindful of His work in your life. We're reminded to not "quench the Spirit" (1 Thessalonians 5:19).

Write what you might be trying to "fix" by yourself. What are you trying to sort out or get through on your own? What have you been doing to try to fix something on your own?

In addition to setting aside the time to call on the power of the Holy Spirit to help you with your daily struggles, think of ways you could remind yourself throughout your day that the power of God is in you. For me, words are powerful, so I write out verses and place them where I can see them during the day. Perhaps you are more visual; if so, you could post some pictures that represent God's power, abundance, creativity, or majesty. You could write on the pictures: "I have [power, beauty, creativity, majesty] in me!" Jot down some ideas for reminding yourself that God has given you a Helper who abides in you:

Next, Jesus told His disciples, "Peace I leave with you; my peace I give to you" (v. 27). Notice that we already have His peace. He does not say that He "might" leave His peace or that it will happen in the future. He already did it: My peace I give to you. So many people today are searching for peace. Even many Christians seem to be in a state of discontent or running around frazzled. A frazzled life is not what Jesus intended for us. He came to give us peace. But also see that He said, "not as the world gives do I give to you."

Let's focus on God's promise of peace. Notice that it is not just any peace. God promised that the "peace of God, which surpasses all understanding, will guard your hearts and minds in Christ Jesus." Read together, John 14:27 and Philippians 4:7 tell us that God's peace is different than something people can manufacture. Jesus said, "Peace I leave with you," but then His very next words were, "My peace I give to you." Why both? In Philippians 4:7, Paul specifically cites the "peace of God, which surpasses all understanding." It *must* be that divine peace is different than any peace we could achieve on our own. Notice that divine peace "will guard your hearts and minds in Christ Jesus." Isn't that what you need? I do. My heart is often hurting and my mind is always racing. I need Jesus to guard my heart *and* my mind. I don't need help with just one or the other, but both my heart and my mind need to be guarded. When I get frazzled, I pray for God to give me His peace, which is beyond my comprehension, to guard my heart and my mind in Jesus. And He does!

Remember that the Word of God is meant to be put into action to change your life. Write how you could call on the peace of God in your daily life:

Notice that chapter 14 essentially opens and closes (see verses 1 and 27) with Jesus telling His disciples, "Let not your hearts be troubled" and "neither let them be afraid." He said it both times in connection with telling His disciples that He was going away. Jesus explained that He would be with us through the Holy Spirit, but He knew that this was a difficult concept to understand and appreciate.

Jesus also added to this passage an instruction on how we are to deal with death and grieving. In verse 28, Jesus gave a gentle reprimand to His disciples. He said, "If you loved me, you would have rejoiced, because I am going to the Father, for the Father is greater than I." Ouch! It seems that the disciples were too focused on themselves and their imminent loss. Jesus directed them to rejoice because He was going to the Father. What a beautiful message to remember as we encounter the loss of loved ones in our lives.

As this chapter closes, note the importance of obedience as an expression of love. Jesus said, "I do as the Father has commanded me, so that the world may know that I love the Father" (v. 31). Jesus had a choice. He did not have to die on that cross. In chapter 13 we discussed that Jesus commanded Judas to "do quickly" what he intended, and here, in verse 30, Jesus said, "the ruler of this world is coming. He has no claim on me."

Read John 10:17–18 and write the passage in your own words:

Jesus was not a victim. He loved the Father so much that He was willing to obey, even to His death. He loved you so much that He was willing to take on your sin, receive your punishment from the Father, and die on that cross. But wait, that's not all (sounds like those commercials: "But wait, there's more!"). By putting your faith in Him, He will dwell in you, the Father will love you, *and* you receive the gift of the Holy Spirit to abide in you. It seems too good to be true, but it's not. God's Word makes it clear that Jesus came to do *all* these things for us. Just take a moment and let that soak into your soul.

> What you have learned and received and heard and seen in me—practice these things, and the God of peace will be with you. —Philippians 4:9

Closing Prayer: Father, Your love for me is overwhelming. Help me understand the depth of Your love and compassion toward me. Help me rely on the Holy Spirit to guide my life, in both my daily choices and major decisions. Lord, I pray for Your peace. I thank You for Jesus and His love for me. I pray that I will obey Your commands and experience the peace that only You can give. Please guard my heart and my mind in my Savior! In Jesus' name I pray. Amen.

REVIEW, REFLECT, AND PRAY

Before you begin today, ask God to reveal anything you may have missed the first time through the lessons. Take time to review the daily verses and fill in any spaces you left blank, if you can. Remember that only God through the Holy Spirit grants understanding, especially when it comes to God's Word. And be assured, it's okay if you have empty spaces.

Read what you wrote about God in each chart and write your thoughts here:

Next, read what you wrote in response to the questions in each lesson and take a few minutes to pray about what God wants you to learn.

If God revealed something to you, write about it here:

If God reminded you of something you've been forgetting lately, or showed you something that hasn't been part of your life for a while, write about it here:

If God challenged you this week to make a change in your life, how did He do it and what change will you make?

Before you end this week, take a few moments to be quiet and still. Take time to let the lessons of this week become wisdom in your heart. Take time to let the Holy Spirit speak to you.

> Do not be anxious about anything, but in everything by prayer and supplication with thanksgiving let your requests be made known to God. And the peace of God, which surpasses all understanding, will guard your hearts and your minds in Christ Jesus. —Philippians 4:6–7

Closing Prayer: Lord, thank You for choosing me and loving me. I pray that I will seek Your will through the Holy Spirit. Help me comprehend that, through my faith, You are in me and I am in You. Help me comprehend that the Father loves me and has equipped me with the Holy Spirit. I pray that my life will reflect my faith in Jesus and the work of the Holy Spirit in me. In Jesus' name I pray. Amen.

JESUS IS THE WAY, THE TRUTH, AND THE LIFE

1. Review the lessons and what you wrote for Day 5. Share insights with the group.

2. Do you truly and sincerely believe in heaven? What do you think it will be like?

3. Discuss a time when your prayers went unanswered. What did you learn from that time in your life?

4. Discuss a time when you knew the Holy Spirit was speaking to you.

5. Is there something in your life for which you should stop asking the Lord for help and start claiming the power of the Holy Spirit, who is already within you?

6. Gather prayer requests for the week and close in prayer.

abide
in Him

JOHN 15

Last week, you read about my skeptical start with my Bible.

Before I gave my life to the Lord Jesus Christ and received the Holy Spirit, I thought the Bible was a rulebook and impossible to follow. I figured if you followed all those rules, life would surely be boring and you would have no fun at all.

In these chapters we are studying, Jesus did say several times to obey His commands. Before Christ came into my life, when I heard these Scriptures, I pictured obedient little children in uniforms, sitting at desks in straight rows, hands folded, and heads bowed. I did not want to be one of them! I actually used to say that I would enjoy hell because I'd see all my friends there. Now I cannot imagine such thoughts. The Lord rescued me from such inaccurate views of Him and His Word. Praise the Lord! I am so grateful and humbled.

Chapter 15 is packed full of amazing truths about the character of our God. You might get the wrong impression on first read, as I did, but ask that the Holy Spirit would reveal God's meaning in this chapter of John's gospel.

As a new believer, reading John 15 knocked my socks off! I couldn't believe I had gotten it so wrong. My prior beliefs were backwards and untrue. I wept over the life I led before Christ because I had wasted so much time thinking that all God did was demand, condemn, and punish. I had no idea how much He loved me. I had no idea that He wanted me to be His friend. I had no idea that He wanted me to believe in Him so I could have His daily presence in the Holy Spirit and eternal life in heaven. I wasted more than thirty-five years of His love, friendship, and fellowship. I lived more than thirty-five years without His help. As I read chapter 15 through the eyes of the Holy Spirit, I began to see, truly see, God's desire for my life.

To "abide" means to continue, to be steadfast, to stay. Jesus told the disciples to abide in Him because He loved them. He desired an intimate relationship with them. It was not a threat! In fact, He went on to call His disciples "friends," and said that there is no greater love than for one to lay down his life for his friends.

Jesus wants you to continue with Him so that He may fill you with the divine joy of His friendship and presence. For the honor of His friendship, what He asks is that you love Him and love one another. It's really that simple. All of the other "rules" I thought God had for us really flow from these two acts of obedience. But as easy as it seems, God knows we cannot do this alone. He knows we need Him or we will fail. Because He loves us, He wants us to abide in Him so we have a fighting chance at loving Him and others. I wish I had understood this truth earlier in life.

> Whatever troubles or hardships we go through, we can count on one thing: the Lord will never leave us or forsake us.

Chapter 15, however, is not all rosy. Jesus warned His followers that the world would persecute them. Jesus explained that those in the world do not know Him or the Father, so they would bring trouble for those who follow Christ. There is no doubt we will experience hardship in this life. Jesus spoke plainly of the tribulation we will face in this world, but we can hold tight to His promises. We will have the Holy Spirit to help us, and when we "abide" in Christ, that is, stay close to Him, He will fill us with divine joy, even through our troubles. In fact, I believe He will fill us with His joy *especially* through our troubles.

When we lost our three-year-old son, I was pretty certain that I would never be truly happy or joyful again. How could I be? There was an enormous hole in my heart that could not be filled or repaired. Or so I thought. Yet, as I grew in my relationship with the Lord, learned more of His truths from the Bible, spent more time in prayer, and began to call on Him to heal me, the Lord slowly restored joy (which could only be His divine joy) and happiness to my heart. Only the Lord could heal this wound. Only the Holy Spirit could pick me up day after day and speak words of hope and comfort to my soul.

Whatever troubles or hardships we go through, we can count on one thing: the Lord will never leave us or forsake us (Hebrews 13:5). As Psalm 34:18 assures us, "The LORD is near to the brokenhearted and saves the crushed in spirit." John 15 explains why this promise holds true.

I hope you are overwhelmed by the everlasting lovingkindness of our God in this week's lessons. It is my prayer that you will be amazed and renewed with a fire to serve a God who loves you so much!

I AM THE VINE,
YOU ARE THE BRANCHES

Read John 15:1–8 in your Bible. Then fill in the chart, verse by verse.

Briefly write what each verse reveals to you about the Father, the Son, or the Holy Spirit. Perhaps the verse reflects a character trait of God (merciful, patient, gentle, loving). The verse might show what the Lord values (obedience, service) or how He wants us to behave (humbly, kindly, compassionately). It's fine to leave some spaces blank since you won't find an answer to the question in every verse. The idea is to read each verse thinking, *Does this verse tell me anything about God?* and then writing what comes to mind.

JOHN 15:1–8	What does this verse tell me about God?
1. "I am the true vine, and my Father is the vinedresser."	
2. "Every branch in me that does not bear fruit he takes away, and every branch that bears fruit he prunes, that it may bear more fruit."	
3. "Already you are clean because of the word that I have spoken to you."	

4. "Abide in me, and I in you. As the branch cannot bear fruit by itself, unless it abides in the vine, neither can you, unless you abide in me."

5. "I am the vine; you are the branches. Whoever abides in me and I in him, he it is that bears much fruit, for apart from me you can do nothing."

6. "If anyone does not abide in me he is thrown away like a branch and withers; and the branches are gathered, thrown into the fire, and burned."

7. "If you abide in me, and my words abide in you, ask whatever you wish, and it will be done for you."

8. "By this my Father is glorified, that you bear much fruit and so prove to be my disciples."

Jesus is the vine and the Father the vinedresser, meaning Jesus is life itself, from whence life flows. The Father, as the vinedresser, is in control.

The next verse is complicated and a bit troublesome at first glance. If we don't bear fruit (what does that mean anyway?), the Father will take us away? And if we *do* bear fruit, the Father will prune us? Neither one sounds appealing on first read. As we search for the deeper meaning, this verse gives us wisdom regarding a couple of important truths. First, faith without action is dead. A branch without fruit will be cut off. You simply cannot be truly committed to the Lord and have faith in Jesus without acting in some way that bears fruit for God's kingdom.

Second, the Father guides our life and our circumstances for good. Even if the pruning is painful and long-suffering, it is meant to grow us in Christ so we may bear more fruit. If we can look at our life troubles as "pruning" for our own good, even when we cannot see it or feel it at the time, we will be an example of Christ to others.

Write about the pruning that has occurred in your life. Describe, if you can, the fruit—results, benefits—that came from it:

Next, Jesus told the disciples again that they were clean. Initially, this sentence seemed out of place to me, especially considering the next several verses. Then the Lord revealed its significance: we cannot earn salvation by our works. Jesus did not want us to think that our fruit was the reason for our salvation. He wanted to be clear—"Already you are clean because of the word that I have spoken to you." So we can bear fruit, and God can prune us and we may bear more fruit. But we should not confuse that with salvation. We are saved by our faith in Christ.

Jesus did go on to tell us how to bear fruit. We are to abide in Him. John, in 1 John 2:4–6, helps us put these verses together: "Whoever says 'I know him' but does not keep his commandments is a liar, and the truth is not in him, but whoever keeps his word, in him the love of God is perfected. By this we may know that we are in him: whoever says he abides in him ought to walk in the same way in which he walked."

Write how you can keep His commandments and His Word. List some practical ways that you can live your life in the same manner as Christ.

Verse 5 of John 15 contains a phrase I often still struggle with: "apart from me you can do nothing." I get so wrapped up in making plans and filling my plate with things to do that I constantly forget I could do *none* of these things without God. Everything I do, I do because He allows it and gives me the ability to do it. I can do nothing apart from Him.

I have always been independent, always been in constant motion. As a new believer, understanding that I am not in control of my life and my circumstances turned me upside down. I had always believed that if you worked hard and did your best, things would go well for you. I had always believed that honesty, hard work, striving for excellence, and working well with others were what led to success. I believed you could do almost anything if you worked hard enough. So, "apart from me you can do nothing," was initially difficult for me. But as I grew in my faith and trust in the Lord, I began to understand His complete command over every aspect of my life.

Write something that you know you could not have done apart from Him:

Take a few moments to reflect. Is it difficult for you to surrender *everything* to God's control? Are you trying to do anything apart from God? Are you pushing to make something happen? Are you encountering difficulties in some area, but forgetting to pray about the situation? Are you seeking God's will, or are you creating your own plan?

Write about something you have been trying to do on your own, apart from God:

Read Matthew 7:7–8 and write down how this passage ties together with John 15:7.

Jesus told the disciples they would glorify the Father and prove to be His disciples when they "bear much fruit." John 8:31–32 says, "So Jesus said to the Jews who had believed him, 'If you abide in my word, you are truly my disciples, and you will know the truth, and the truth will set you free.'" These verses tell us how important it is to live in a way that represents Christ and His Word. Keep studying the Word, keep praying, keep seeking the Holy Spirit, and keep trying to live more like Christ. It will set you free!

"Let your light shine before others, so that they may see your good works and give glory to your Father who is in heaven." —Matthew 5:16

Closing Prayer: Father in heaven, help me to abide in You and bear much fruit for Your glory. Lord, my heart's desire is to be one of Your disciples. Help me accept those times when You will allow pruning in my life for my benefit and for the benefit of Your kingdom. Allow understanding to become wisdom within me so my reactions to the trials in life set an example for others. Father, thank You for setting me free in Your Word and in the precious name of Your Son, Jesus Christ. Help me use this divine freedom to shine a light to lead others to You. In Jesus' name I pray. Amen.

GREATER LOVE HAS NO ONE THAN THIS

Read John 15:9–15 in your Bible.
Then fill in the chart, verse by verse.

Briefly write what each verse reveals to you about the Father, the Son, or the Holy Spirit. Perhaps the verse reflects a character trait of God (merciful, patient, gentle, loving). The verse might show what the Lord values (obedience, service) or how He wants us to behave (humbly, kindly, compassionately). It's fine to leave some spaces blank since you won't find an answer to the question in every verse. The idea is to read each verse thinking, *Does this verse tell me anything about God?* and then writing what comes to mind.

JOHN 15:9–15	What does this verse tell me about God?
9. "As the Father has loved me, so I have loved you. Abide in my love."	
10. "If you keep my commandments, you will abide in my love, just as I have kept my Father's commandments and abide in his love."	
11. "These things I have spoken to you, that my joy may be in you, and that your joy may be full."	

12. "This is my commandment, that you love one another as I have loved you."

13. "Greater love has no one than this, that someone lay down his life for his friends."

14. "You are my friends if you do what I command you."

15. "No longer do I call you servants, for the servant does not know what his master is doing; but I have called you friends, for all that I have heard from my Father I have made known to you."

Love, Love, Love! These verses are filled with love. Something that struck me while writing this lesson was that Jesus repeatedly instructed the disciples to keep His Word and keep His commandments . . . to abide in Him. Yet, look closely. He did not say these things to exhibit His power, His authority, or His control over us. He wants us to keep His commandments because He *loves* us! The Creator of the universe loves you so much that He wants you to abide in Him so He can abide in you. He wants you to obey out of love, not fear, control, or power, but out of love. Jesus asked that you love Him by obeying Him.

Next, Jesus told the disciples why He wanted them to show love for Him through obedience: "that my joy may be in you, and that your joy may be full." Not for His benefit . . . but for *their* joy! And not just some ordinary joy, but to be full of *His* joy, overflowing with divine joy. Unbelievable. Keeping His commands is starting to sound better and better, isn't it? Keeping His commands will set us free, our joy will be made full, He will abide in us and love us . . . sounds worth striving for, doesn't it?

Read Ephesians 3:17–19 and put the passage into your own words:

Christ wants to dwell in your heart so you will know how wide and long and high and deep is His love for you *and* so you may be filled up with the "fullness of God." When was the last time your joy was made full? When was the last time you felt the fullness of God overflowing in your life?

If what you wrote above didn't happen within the last month, please take time to consider the verses in today's lesson. Let these truths sink into your heart. It is God's desire for you to have joy and fullness in Him. If you are not experiencing His joy and fullness on a regular, daily basis, what is stopping you? Are you trying to get through life "apart from Him"? Are you spending enough time with Him? Slow down today and let Him fill you up. If you work outside the home, take a half day off. If you stay at home with children, call for help and get away for a few hours. Instead of cleaning up or doing laundry after the kids go to school, spend time in prayer and in His Word. Let Him speak to you in His lovingkindness so you can see if you are not abiding in Him in some way. I will pray for you to feel the presence of the Lord and His astounding, never-ending love for you.

One of my favorite verses is John 15:13 because it speaks volumes about God's character. It is amazing that God would call us friends and lay down His life for us. I recall reading this for the first time and thinking, *Yes!* There is no greater love than a friend who would lay down his life for you.

Do you have a friend (not your family or your spouse) who would lay down her life for you? If you said yes, do you know how rare and amazing that friendship is? Do you know how deep that friendship must run? Do you appreciate how much that person must love you? If you said yes, please take a moment to thank God for that person in your life. Next, make a note to spend some time with that friend this week. If you said no or you were not sure, here's the great news . . . you *do* have such a friend! It's Jesus. He calls you friend *and* He already offered His life for you. You can spend as much time with Him as you want this week!

Read Matthew 12:50 and think about John 15:13 again. What do these Scriptures tell you about the character of God? What do these verses tell you about how God thinks of you and your relationship with Him?

We end our lesson today in verse 15 when Jesus told the disciples that He had spoken from the Father and that He had shared with them, as friends, "all" that He heard from the Father. What did Jesus tell them? It was all about His love and the Father's love for them. Abide in Him. Show your love for Him by being obedient. Be filled with joy!

It is a very simple, beautiful message. Was there a time when you thought a relationship with God, let alone a friendship with God, was more complicated than these verses explain? Did you ever think that you had to earn His love? Was there ever a time when you *didn't* know He loved you so much? Write about it here:

Now, take a moment and thank God for saving you through Christ. Pause and praise God for growing your faith and relationship with Him so you can now see His love and appreciate His simple truth that our love for Him is all He requires of us.

Now I ask you, dear lady—not as though I were writing you a new commandment, but the one we have had from the beginning—that we love one another. —2 John 5

Closing Prayer: Dear Lord Jesus, that You would call me friend and lay down Your life for me is more than I deserve. It is difficult for me to comprehend. Father, help me know Your divine love and share it with others. My prayer is that I will abide in You and keep Your commands. I pray that I will call on the Holy Spirit to help me obey Your Word. My desire is for my life to be in obedience to You, Father, and that I might be filled with Your joy and the fullness of the Holy Spirit. In the name of the triune God, I pray. Amen.

I CHOSE YOU OUT OF THE WORLD

Read John 15:16–20 in your Bible.
Next, complete the chart below, verse by verse.

Briefly write what each verse reveals to you about the Father, the Son, or the Holy Spirit. Perhaps the verse reflects a character trait of God (merciful, patient, gentle, loving). The verse might show what the Lord values (obedience, service) or how He wants us to behave (humbly, kindly, compassionately). It's fine to leave some spaces blank since you won't find an answer to the question in every verse. The idea is to read each verse thinking, *Does this verse tell me anything about God?* and then writing what comes to mind.

JOHN 15:16–20	What does this verse tell me about God?
16. "You did not choose me, but I chose you and appointed you that you should go and bear fruit and that your fruit should abide, so that whatever you ask the Father in my name, he may give it to you."	
17. "These things I command you, so that you will love one another."	
18. "If the world hates you, know that it has hated me before it hated you."	

19. "If you were of the world, the world would love you as its own; but because you are not of the world, but I chose you out of the world, therefore the world hates you."

20. "Remember the word that I said to you: 'A servant is not greater than his master.' If they persecuted me, they will also persecute you. If they kept my word, they will also keep yours."

Verse 16 says, "I chose you." That nearly makes me weep. He *wants* me. He wants *me*! He also appointed me to do His work, to bear fruit. And, by the way, whatever I ask in His name, the Father may give it to me. What? Why me? What's so special about me that the God of the universe would choose to die for me? I still have no idea, but it doesn't matter. He did.

What matters now is what I choose to do with this divine appointment. What will you do with it? I know it's a big question, but try to write about it. I'll give you some extra time and space! Consider what gifts the Lord has given you. Consider what you think God would have you do to build or help His kingdom. It's okay to brainstorm and write several ideas or thoughts here.

Now that we have taken a moment to marvel at our divine appointment and reflect about what we will do, let's look at what might get in our way. Look at verses 18–19 again and then read 1 John 3:13. What do these verses say we will face from the world?

Take hope! Matthew 10:22 says, "You will be hated by all for my name's sake. But the one who endures to the end will be saved." First Corinthians 4:12 says it this way: "We labor, working with our own hands. When reviled, we bless; when persecuted, we endure." And Jesus said, "Truly, truly, I say to you, if anyone keeps my word, he will never see death" (John 8:51, meaning eternal separation from Him).

What obstacles are you facing as you carry out your divine appointment? For example, do you have an unbelieving or unsupportive spouse? A difficult work environment? Cliques at church? Too many family obligations?

I take heart in John 15:19: "You are not of the world, but I chose you out of the world." When I face obstacles and trials in what I believe God is calling me to do, I try to remember that as a Christian, I am no longer "of this world" because He, the Creator, chose me out of the world. Whatever the trouble may be, it is not bigger than God. Whatever the trouble may be, it is only "of this world," and it cannot stop me if God has called me to do it. When you encounter trouble from the world, remember this:

> Persecuted, but not forsaken; struck down, but not destroyed; . . . For this light momentary affliction is preparing for us an eternal weight of glory beyond all comparison. —2 Corinthians 4:9, 17

Closing Prayer: Father, I am humbled that You chose me out of this world. I pray that I will honor You as I carry out my divine appointment to bear fruit for Your glory. Lord, show me Your will for my life so I know what to ask in Your name. Help me endure and persevere in Your name and in keeping Your Word. Help me understand that because they persecuted You, they will persecute me. Lord, help me to bear any affliction associated with Your name because I know it is for Your purpose and Your eternal glory. In Jesus' name I pray. Amen.

WEEK 3 | DAY 4

THEY DO NOT KNOW THE ONE WHO SENT ME

Read John 15:21–27 in your Bible.
Next, complete the chart below, verse by verse.

Briefly write what each verse reveals to you about the Father, the Son, or the Holy Spirit. Perhaps the verse reflects a character trait of God (merciful, patient, gentle, loving). The verse might show what the Lord values (obedience, service) or how He wants us to behave (humbly, kindly, compassionately). It's fine to leave some spaces blank since you won't find an answer to the question in every verse. The idea is to read each verse thinking, *Does this verse tell me anything about God?* and then writing what comes to mind.

JOHN 15:21–27	What does this verse tell me about God?
21. "But all these things they will do to you on account of my name, because they do not know him who sent me."	
22. "If I had not come and spoken to them, they would not have been guilty of sin, but now they have no excuse for their sin."	
23. "He who hates me hates my Father also."	

24. "If I had not done among them
the works that no one else did,
they would not be guilty of sin,
but now they have seen and hated
both me and my Father."

25. "But the word that is written
in their Law must be fulfilled:
'They hated me without a cause.'"

26. "But when the Helper comes,
whom I will send to you from the
Father, the Spirit of truth, who
proceeds from the Father, he will
bear witness about me."

27. "And you also will bear
witness, because you have been
with me from the beginning."

Early in the church, as the disciples began to spread the gospel, Peter and John
healed a man and everyone saw the healed man praising God. Peter told them that
God healed the man through Jesus Christ. The elders of the temple in Jerusalem
began to talk about the miracle:

> What shall we do with these men [Peter and John]? For that a notable
> sign has been performed through them is evident to all the inhabitants
> of Jerusalem, and we cannot deny it. But in order that it may spread no
> further among the people, let us warn them to speak no more to anyone
> in this name. —Acts 4:16–17

Doing work for the glory of Christ often draws attention, criticism, or resistance. Are you getting any resistance or questioning from those around you about your divine appointment? Do you ever feel hesitant to share the gospel and tell people about your faith in Jesus Christ?

Write about these situations. Who is giving you resistance or trying to stand in your way? When do you feel hesitant to share your faith?

Let's look at what happened next to Peter and John:

> So they [the elders] called them and charged them not to speak or teach at all in the name of Jesus. But Peter and John answered them, "Whether it is right in the sight of God to listen to you rather than to God, you must judge, for we cannot but speak of what we have seen and heard." —Acts 4:18–20

Can you be this bold for Christ? Do you want to know what happened next? We see in verse 21 that the elders threatened them with punishment, but they let them go on account of all the people glorifying God for the miracle of healing the man.

Press forward in whatever God is calling you to do. You will encounter resistance, but if you are doing God's will, He will be glorified by your actions. I love what Peter and John did next. They gathered together and lifted their voices to God and asked for help! They asked for God to give them confidence to heal and to do wonders in the name of Jesus. The place where they gathered was shaken and they were filled with the Holy Spirit. They began to speak the word of God with boldness (Acts 4:23–31).

Take a moment now and pray about the resistance you wrote about above. Ask God to remove it. Ask God to give you confidence to boldly do what He has put on your heart, regardless of whether or not He removes your resistance. Read 1 Peter 4:12–19 and put this passage into your own words:

Let's consider the alternative in verses 21–24: "they do not know him who sent me" or they "hated both me and my Father." Having seen and heard about Jesus and the works He did, "now they have no excuse for their sin." Even if times get more difficult, and we begin to see more persecution of Christians, and even if I face it myself, I would rather endure and persevere in Jesus' name than be one of the people facing the alternative described in Scripture.

Look back at Week 2, Day 1 (page 53) where you wrote the names of three people you know who have not put their faith in Jesus Christ as their Savior. Write their names again and pray about each one. Ask the Father to soften their hearts and turn their souls to Christ. Ask that the Holy Spirit would reveal if you are to take any actions to lead them closer to Jesus. If the Holy Spirit puts something on your heart, write about it here, and make a commitment to take action in obedience to Him.

Through the tribulations we will surely face, we cannot miss the great gift we receive as believers. Once again Jesus told the disciples about the Helper, the Spirit of Truth, who proceeds from the Father and whom Jesus sends to us. As I encounter resistance and trials in my daily life, I am trying to make it a habit to stop and seek the help of the Holy Spirit to guide me in my actions. Consider for a moment how often you ask for and are aware of the Holy Spirit's help during each day and choose one:

☐ In the morning during prayer time, but not much after that

☐ All the time, often throughout my day

☐ Sometimes, but not often

☐ Rarely

☐ Never

First Thessalonians 5 tells us to "pray continually" and also to not "quench the Spirit" (vv. 17, 19). Ask the Lord to show you some practical ways you can pray without ceasing during the day. And ask Him to show you the Holy Spirit's working in your life, remembering that He is your Counselor, Helper, Advocate, Intercessor, Guide, Teacher. Write down what He puts in your heart and mind to help make you more aware of the Holy Spirit's working in your life.

As we close this week's lessons, let's meditate on what Jesus said to His disciples, "you also will bear witness, because you have been with me from the beginning." Write what you think Jesus meant by this statement:

I pray that each of us will be bold for Christ and be confident to spread the good news of Christ our Savior.

> By this we know that we abide in him and he in us, because he has given us of his Spirit. And we have seen and testify that the Father has sent his Son to be the Savior of the world. Whoever confesses that Jesus is the Son of God, God abides in him, and he in God. —1 John 4:13–15

> We have come to know and to believe the love that God has for us. God is love, and whoever abides in love abides in God, and God abides in him. —1 John 4:16

Closing Prayer: Lord, I praise and worship You. Thank You for calling me to know You and the Father. Help me to call on the magnificent gift of the Helper in my daily life so I may serve Jesus and live for His glory. Father, I pray that I will testify boldly and with confidence about Jesus, our Savior. In Jesus' name I pray. Amen.

REVIEW, REFLECT, AND PRAY

Before you begin today, ask God to reveal anything you may have missed the first time through the lessons. Take time to reread John 15 and fill in any spaces you left blank, if you can. Remember that only God through the Holy Spirit grants understanding, especially when it comes to God's Word. It's okay if you have empty spaces.

Read what you wrote about God in each chart and write your thoughts here:

Next, read what you wrote in response to the questions in each lesson and take a few minutes to pray about what God wants you to learn.

If God revealed something to you this week, write about it here:

If God reminded you of something you've been forgetting lately, or showed you something that hasn't been part of your life for a while, write about it here:

If God challenged you this week to make a change in your life, how did He do it and what change will you make?

Before you end this week, take a few moments to be quiet and still. Take time to let the lessons become wisdom in your heart. Take time to sit in praise and worship of Him and His amazing love.

> No one has ever seen God; if we love one another, God abides in us and his love is perfected in us. —1 John 4:12

Closing Prayer: Father, help me use what I am learning in this study in my daily life. I want to be transformed in my heart so my actions speak boldly of You and Your never-ending love for us. Help me to be patient with those who do not yet know You, with an understanding that they do not have the privilege of knowing You. Help me recognize throughout my day that You abide in me, and I abide in You. Lord, help me comprehend this amazing relationship with You and put it into action in my relationships with others. In Jesus' name I pray. Amen.

DISCUSSION GUIDE | WEEK THREE: JOHN 15

ABIDE IN HIM

1. Review the lessons and what you wrote for Day 5. Share insights with the group.

2. Describe a time of pruning and the fruit that came from that time in your life.

3. Do you consider yourself a friend of Jesus? Why or why not?

4. What obstacles are blocking you from pursuing what God has asked you to do? Perhaps your group can brainstorm ideas for you to overcome these obstacles (in addition to prayer, of course).

5. Discuss the most recent time you shared the gospel message with someone.

6. Gather prayer requests for the week and close in prayer.

filled with the Holy Spirit

JOHN 16

In John 16, Jesus mentions joy several times.

Twice He told the disciples that their grief would be turned to joy. Jesus told them when they see Him again, their hearts would rejoice and "no one will take your joy from you." Jesus also told the disciples to pray that their "joy may be full." At the end of this chapter, Jesus explained that He was telling the disciples all this so that "you may have peace." Grief turned to joy, hearts rejoicing, and peace in this world. All because the Father loves us. All because we believe in Jesus as Lord and Savior. Jesus died to give us all of these things. Yet how much joy, rejoicing, and peace surrounds your daily life?

As a grieving mother, I cling to these verses. At times, the only way I could even lift my head was to remember these verses. I would repeat His promises until the pain subsided: My grief *will* be turned into joy. My heart *will* rejoice because I *will* get to see my son again when I get to see Jesus in heaven. As long as I have the Helper, the Spirit of Truth, no one and *nothing* can take my joy from me. Despite a heavy heart, with the power and presence of my God, I *will* live a joyful life. I *will* have peace in this world while I wait to laugh and play with my son again . . . You get the idea!

I think many of us take joy and peace too lightly. Perhaps the words become too familiar to truly grasp the magnificent promises in this week's lessons. True joy that fills you up and spills out of you onto others is a blessing from God. You know it when you experience it. You feel it when you encounter others who are full of joy. When you are filled with joy through Christ, others will take note of you. When you let no one take your joy from you—no matter what—others wonder about you. This is one area where you *want* people to talk about you: "Why is she so joyful all the time?" "How can she be so positive right now?"

> **Jesus promised both peace and joy to us.**
> **Why would we live any other way?**

When you have tribulation, you can have peace because you know that Jesus has overcome the world. When you rest your soul in His victory, peace will flow through you, but it will also flow around you. Peace is another quality that people take note of when they encounter it in someone. Especially in times of trouble, when you hold on to the peace of God, people will be amazed: "Where does she get her strength?" "I don't know how she does it. I would fall apart."

Joy and peace seem to be so rare in our world that folks think both are unusual. For the Christian, both should be sought after each and every day. Why? Because people will talk about you. People will wonder what you have that they don't. If you exhibit joy and peace, people will *want* what you have and start asking how to get it. Joy and peace lived out in our everyday lives are the lights that lead others to Christ.

Jesus promised both peace and joy to us. Why would we live any other way? What's our excuse for allowing something or someone to take it from us? Is whatever is "stealing" our peace or joy important enough to allow it to get in the way of showing others the love of God?

If something or someone is stealing your joy or your peace, the enemy is having a great and powerful impact. Instead of shedding light, you are giving the enemy more ammunition for his spiritual warfare. When we don't live the joyful and peaceful life Jesus died to give us, we let the enemy win.

We simply must decide, every single day, to *choose* joy and peace. Choose joy for the sake of leading others to God. Choose it for Christ. Choose it because God chose to make you His! Don't waste His precious gift of His Son and the Holy Spirit.

You cannot do this alone. You cannot live a life so filled with joy and peace that others recognize something different in you without the power of the Holy Spirit flowing through you. If you are having a difficult, irritable, angry, or frustrating day, stop and ask that the Holy Spirit will rise up and help you fight. Ask the Spirit of Truth, your Helper, to fill you up with divine joy and peace. Be filled with the Holy Spirit, not the things of this world. If you feel like you are failing at peace and joy, then open your Bible! Read chapter 16 again and again until you feel like shouting it from the rooftops. God deserves our best, and the best way to lead others to Him is to live a life of peace and joy. I pray that this week's lessons help you choose both joy and peace every day.

WEEK 4 | DAY 1

THE HELPER

Read John 16:1–11 in your Bible.
Next, complete the chart below, verse by verse.

Briefly write what each verse reveals to you about the Father, the Son, or the Holy Spirit. Perhaps the verse reflects a character trait of God (merciful, patient, gentle, loving). The verse might show what the Lord values (obedience, service) or how He wants us to behave (humbly, kindly, compassionately). It's fine to leave some spaces blank since you won't find an answer to the question in every verse. The idea is to read each verse thinking, *Does this verse tell me anything about God?* and then writing what comes to mind.

JOHN 16:1–11	What does this verse tell me about God?
1. "I have said all these things to you to keep you from falling away."	
2. "They will put you out of the synagogues. Indeed, the hour is coming when whoever kills you will think he is offering service to God."	
3. "And they will do these things because they have not known the Father, nor me."	

What does this verse tell me about God?

4. "But I have said these things to you, that when their hour comes you may remember that I told them to you. I did not say these things to you from the beginning, because I was with you."

5. "But now I am going to him who sent me, and none of you asks me, 'Where are you going?'"

6. "But because I have said these things to you, sorrow has filled your heart."

7. "Nevertheless, I tell you the truth: it is to your advantage that I go away, for if I do not go away, the Helper will not come to you. But if I go, I will send him to you."

8. "And when he comes, he will convict the world concerning sin and righteousness and judgment:"

9. "concerning sin, because they do not believe in me;"

10. "concerning righteousness, because I go to the Father and you will see me no longer;"

11. "concerning judgment, because the ruler of this world is judged."

Jesus knew this time was going to be difficult for the disciples, and He loved them. Jesus was warning the disciples of things to come. He was trying to explain why these things would happen, "because they have not known the Father, nor me." He was also trying to warn them so that they would "be kept from falling away." Another translation renders this verse "be kept from stumbling" (NASB).

A good example of stumbling is found in John 9:17–23. Read that passage now.

Jesus healed a man who was born blind. Trying to get to the bottom of this miracle, which was "unlawfully" performed on a Sabbath, the Pharisees questioned the blind man's parents. What did the parents say? Why did the parents say what they did?

I like to think that I would react differently. I like to believe that I would not have denied that Christ healed my child who had been blind his whole life. I would shout about Jesus from the rooftops! I'd tell everyone I know. I'd become His greatest, most loyal follower . . . and on and on.

But how often in my daily life do I deny Christ in a similar way? How often does a situation present itself for me to share my faith, but I do not? How many times have I failed to show someone the love of Christ? How often do I go through the day without shouting His name in joy because of all the blessings I have received? List a few ways that you have been "stumbling" in your faith walk:

We will face difficulties or some things that make us outcasts in this world because of our faith in Christ. Ask God to forgive you for the fear of being an outcast in His name. Ask the Holy Spirit to strengthen you to proclaim His name and your faith boldly among others. Also, keep in mind that others may treat you poorly because they do not know the Father or Jesus (John 8:19; John 15:21; John 16:3).

Jesus recognized and acknowledged that sorrow had filled the hearts of His disciples. What troubles have filled you with sorrow?

Sometimes, especially when sorrow fills our hearts, we can forget the next part of the message. Jesus assured the disciples that it was to their advantage if He went away because then the Helper would be sent to them. I have struggled with this. How could being apart from Jesus be to the disciples' advantage? Think about that for just a moment. What could be better than being in the presence of Jesus? Remember that until Jesus died on the cross for our sins, we were separated from God. Jesus assured us that when He returned to the Father, He would send the Holy Spirit. Reread John 14:16–23. Write what this Scripture says about the Holy Spirit and the nature of our relationship with Jesus and the Father:

Second Timothy 1:7 (NASB) tells us, "for God has not given us a spirit of timidity, but of power and love and discipline." Ask God to help you call on the help of the

Holy Spirit today. You might need help to be bold for Christ. You could ask for help with the discipline to eat in a healthy manner. You might need help with your temper or impatience. You may need help with your sense of peace and trust in the Lord. Write what you will call on the Holy Spirit's help with today:

We've spent some time looking at how we could feel like an outcast and how we could use more help from the Holy Spirit, but before we close, take heart in the last phrase of today's passage: ". . . the ruler of this world is judged." In John 12:31, Jesus had previously taught, "Now is the judgment of this world; now will the ruler of this world be cast out." What do these verses say to you? How do you react?

Whatever others might do to you, whatever people may say about you that makes you feel like an outcast, whatever fear overtakes you when you consider sharing your faith, whatever flaws you may experience in this world, remember that Jesus overcame it all. We do not belong to this world. We belong to Him. Acts 17:30–31 says, "The times of ignorance God overlooked, but now he commands all people everywhere to repent, because he has fixed a day on which he will judge the world in righteousness by a man whom he has appointed; and of this he has given assurance to all by raising him from the dead."

Be bold for Christ; be bold!

"I have said these things to you, that in me you may have peace. In the world you will have tribulation. But take heart; I have overcome the world." —John 16:33

Closing Prayer: Father, thank You for understanding our struggles and our difficulties in this world. Thank You for casting these troubles aside through Jesus. Help me to call on the help of the Holy Spirit to discover Your truths and to be bold for You in my everyday life. I want others to see that I live for You and through You. I want to let Your light shine through me. Heavenly Father, it is my deepest desire to be bold for You and for Your kingdom. Please let the strength to do that overflow within me and show me how You want me to declare Your truth to the world. In Jesus' name I pray. Amen.

WEEK 4 | DAY 2

FROM THE FATHER

Read John 16:12–20 in your Bible.
Next, complete the chart below, verse by verse.

Briefly write what each verse reveals to you about the Father, the Son, or the Holy Spirit. Perhaps the verse reflects a character trait of God (merciful, patient, gentle, loving). The verse might show what the Lord values (obedience, service) or how He wants us to behave (humbly, kindly, compassionately). It's fine to leave some spaces blank since you won't find an answer to the question in every verse. The idea is to read each verse thinking, *Does this verse tell me anything about God?* and then writing what comes to mind.

John 16:12–20	What does this verse tell me about God?
12. "I still have many things to say to you, but you cannot bear them now."	
13. When the Spirit of truth comes, he will guide you into all the truth, for he will not speak on his own authority, but whatever he hears he will speak, and he will declare to you the things that are to come."	
14. "He will glorify me, for he will take what is mine and will declare it to you."	

15. "All that the Father has is mine; therefore I said that he will take what is mine and declare it to you."

16. "A little while, and you will see me no longer; and again a little while, and you will see me."

17. So some of his disciples said to one another, "What is this that he says to us, 'A little while, and you will not see me, and again a little while, and you will see me'; and, 'because I am going to the Father'?"

18. So they were saying, "What does he mean by 'a little while'? We do not know what he is talking about."

19. Jesus knew that they wanted to ask him, so he said to them, "Is this what you are asking yourselves, what I meant by saying, 'A little while and you will not see me, and again a little while and you will see me'?"

20. "Truly, truly, I say to you, you will weep and lament, but the world will rejoice. You will be sorrowful, but your sorrow will turn into joy."

Yesterday, you wrote about what was causing you sorrow. Do not miss the first verse for today. Jesus understands your sorrow and He knows what you can bear and what you cannot. Write a short prayer of praise and gratitude for His compassion for you.

In our verses today, Jesus again promises the gift of the Holy Spirit—the Spirit of truth. What an amazing promise! Verses 13–15 explain some of the functions of the Holy Spirit. Spend some time in these verses today. Reread them, repeat them out loud, journal about them, meditate on them. Ask the Lord to reveal His knowledge to you today. Ask Him for wisdom and understanding about the nature of your relationship with Him and the Holy Spirit. These are powerful truths. If you can make these verses wisdom in your heart, it will change your life from the inside out!

A deep understanding of these three verses is so critical that I want us to spend much of today's lesson on them. Study them, be still before the Lord, and then write what comes to your heart and mind.

John 16:13

John 16:14

Let's move on to verse 16, when Jesus told the disciples that soon they would not see Him, but then a while later they would see Him again. Recall that Jesus told the disciples that they should be glad for Him because "I am going to the Father, for the Father is greater than I" (John 14:28). Jesus was trying to make it clear to the disciples that He was sent from the Father and would return to the Father.

But the disciples just weren't getting it! They were questioning each other about what He meant. Jesus had spoken of His death and resurrection before, when the disciples were traveling to Galilee, but they did not understand: "He was teaching his disciples, saying to them, 'The Son of Man is going to be delivered into the hands of men, and they will kill him. And when he is killed, after three days he will rise.' But they did not understand the saying, and were afraid to ask him" (Mark 9:31–32). In both John 16 and Mark 9, the disciples did not want to question Jesus about what He was telling them. Think of a time when you had a question about something someone told you, but you did not want to ask him or her about it. What made you hesitate to ask? Recall what fears you had at that time. Write why you think the disciples discussed Jesus' words among themselves, but were afraid to question Him about what He was saying:

Of course, eventually, when the timing was right, Jesus would answer their questions and grant them understanding. First, however, He told them what His death and resurrection would do for them—"Your sorrow will turn into joy!" I think this promise relates not only to salvation and eternal life, but also to verses 13–15 and the promise of the Holy Spirit while we spend our time in this world. Although we will grieve in this world, the Holy Spirit will be with us, and one of the fruits of the Holy Spirit is joy.

If we can grasp today's verses, then our lives will change in dramatic and powerful ways. When others see our changed lives, we are shining the light toward Christ. If we truly comprehend and believe that Jesus was of the Father, from the Father, and returned to the Father, then we can put our faith and trust in Him and not in the things of this world. As a result of our faith in Jesus, we are gifted with the Holy Spirit and we can live by the fruit of the Spirit with love, joy, peace, patience, kindness, goodness, faithfulness, gentleness, and self-control (Galatians 5:22–23).

I know that I could use more love, joy, peace, patience, kindness, goodness, faithfulness, gentleness, and self-control in my life! In fact, after preparing this lesson, I began to add Galatians 5:22–23 to my prayers every morning. It reminds me that I can live a life that reflects all of these beautiful things *if* I rely on the Holy Spirit to guide me as I go through my day. My prayer is that my heart is changing from the inside out in a beautiful and recognizable way.

> If we live by the Spirit, let us also keep in step with the Spirit.
> —Galatians 5:25

Closing Prayer: Father, all of the glory and praise belong to You. Your amazing power, combined with Your great love for me, is difficult to comprehend sometimes. Lord, make these precious words and promises wisdom in my heart so I may live each day by the fruit of the Spirit. Help me start my day by acknowledging Your Holy Spirit within me. Help me rely on Your Holy Spirit as I go through my day. Help me end each day with gratitude and praise for Your Holy Spirit who guides my every way. Lord, it is my prayer that my life will be led by the Holy Spirit and that my life will serve Your kingdom and glorify You. In Jesus' name I pray. Amen.

WEEK 4 | DAY 3

THE FATHER LOVES YOU

Read John 16:21–27 in your Bible.
Next, complete the chart below, verse by verse.

Briefly write what each verse reveals to you about the Father, the Son, or the Holy Spirit. Perhaps the verse reflects a character trait of God (merciful, patient, gentle, loving). The verse might show what the Lord values (obedience, service) or how He wants us to behave (humbly, kindly, compassionately). It's fine to leave some spaces blank since you won't find an answer to the question in every verse. The idea is to read each verse thinking, *Does this verse tell me anything about God?* and then writing what comes to mind.

JOHN 16:21–27	What does this verse tell me about God?
21. "When a woman is giving birth, she has sorrow because her hour has come, but when she has delivered the baby, she no longer remembers the anguish, for joy that a human being has been born into the world."	
22. "So also you have sorrow now, but I will see you again, and your hearts will rejoice, and no one will take your joy from you."	
23. "In that day you will ask nothing of me. Truly, truly, I say to you, whatever you ask of the Father in my name, he will give it to you."	

24. "Until now you have asked nothing in my name. Ask, and you will receive, that your joy may be full."

25. "I have said these things to you in figures of speech. The hour is coming when I will no longer speak to you in figures of speech but will tell you plainly about the Father."

26. "In that day you will ask in my name, and I do not say to you that I will ask the Father on your behalf;"

27. "for the Father himself loves you, because you have loved me and have believed that I came from God."

Jesus knew that sorrow had filled His disciples' hearts. Jesus knew they were grieving even what they did not understand fully—that He would be taken from them. But He was reassuring them. It would be similar to childbirth, He told them. You will have pain, but then you will have joy. You will grieve, but then your grief will be turned into joy. One of my favorite verses is, "I will see you again, and your hearts will rejoice, and no one will take your joy from you" (John 16:22).

One thing that Jesus' death and resurrection means is that the Holy Spirit will be sent as our Helper. No one and nothing can take the Holy Spirit away from you if you have accepted Christ as your Lord and Savior! Knowing this amazing truth, how could anyone or anything on this earth take your joy away from you?

Yet many of us who know this awesome truth do not live in this blessing. How many things in life "steal our joy"? How many things do we let irritate us, ruin our day, make us annoyed or angry?

Write some things that happened this week that got in the way of your having a joyful day:

A quote often attributed to Eleanor Roosevelt is "No one can make you feel inferior without your consent." Many years before I came to know the Lord, I learned the truth of this statement. My understanding began with my self-esteem and my feelings of inferiority. I wrote this quote on a piece of paper and kept it folded in my pocket to remind me to be confident.

Several years later, I began to understand that no one can make me feel *anything* without my consent. No one *makes* me angry. No one *makes* me feel happy. I am responsible for my feelings and my emotions, no one else. What an amazing transformation this discovery had on my life! I decided to change and take control of my happiness. It began slowly, one day at a time. Not letting other people or outside circumstances "make" you happy or sad or proud or defeated or angry or irritated takes practice. Implementing a life-changing habit takes acknowledgment of a problem and your responsibility with respect to the problem—and then practice at changing your behavior.

I made part of this transformation before I came to know Jesus as my Savior. I thought of it as the "power of positive thinking." No one can make me be negative without my consent, I was learning, so I chose to be positive. Now, as a Christian empowered with the Holy Spirit and not just my own ability to "think positively,"

I feel even more passionate about this concept. As believers in Christ, we have that same power of God within us. No one can take our joy away from us, unless we allow it.

Emotions are a real part of us; they are God-given, though we must not let emotions override the facts of who we are in Christ or how the Holy Spirit is working in us. Joy and a happy mood are not necessarily the same thing. If we are feeling a certain "bad" way, it could be that we are not living by the fruit of the Spirit; it could be that we are not resting in the powerful promises of God.

Please understand that I am not saying we must never cry or grieve or just have sad moments or even tough seasons. There are times to cry and times to sit with another who's in pain (see Romans 12:15; Ecclesiastes 3:4). My point is that as children of God, we need to strive to keep this world in perspective. Whatever we go through in this life is only temporary, while our relationship with God is eternal. Often our trials bring us closer to the Lord, as it is the hard times that drive us to our knees before Him. While we may be going through a difficult time, as 2 Corinthians 4:16–18 reminds us, these times will pass, and we know that we will spend eternity worshiping God in His glory.

Take a moment to reflect on the things you wrote above and consider whether any of them will have an impact on your eternal life with our Father in heaven. Write about what comes to you while you consider the impact of those things that are stealing your joy:

If you want to make a change toward leading a joyful life, try to recognize when you are not experiencing joy. Then consider whether the person or circumstances that are stealing your joy have any spiritual, eternal impact. If not, release the situation to the Lord and do not allow it to steal your joy! God sent Jesus so that our joy may be made full (John 16:24). Can others see your joy? If not, consider writing John 16:22 on a piece of paper that you can carry with you as a tangible reminder that you have the power of God within you to help you live a joyful life.

Before we finish today, do you see what Jesus explained next? Once we truly believe in Jesus and understand who He is, He will no longer have to act as our intercessor because "the Father himself loves you, because you have loved me and have believed that I came from God" (John 16: 27). This verse overwhelmed me the first time I read it. I think my faith in Jesus finally hit home—because I love Jesus, the Father Himself loves me. The Creator of the universe *loves* me. That He would even know my name would be enough, but He *loves* me. Wow. You could have knocked me over with a feather the first time I let this beautiful truth sink deep into my heart.

How about you? Have you ever really taken it into your heart that the Creator of the universe loves you? The one, true, great, and almighty God *loves* you. Let that settle deep in your soul and see if it doesn't change your life in a powerful way!

> "For the Father himself loves you, because you have loved me and have believed that I came from God." —John 16:27

Closing Prayer: Father, I am humbled that You would love me and care about my joy. It is difficult for me to fully appreciate that You love me in such a way. Please help me understand how much You love me so that when others see me, they can see Your love. I want to live in a way that shows others how faith in Jesus leads to joy. Help me realize when I am allowing the things of this world to steal the joy that Jesus died to give me. Lord, I want to focus on what is important to You so others can see how much I love You. Thank You, Jesus, for showing me the Father's love! In Jesus' name I pray. Amen.

BELIEVE!

Read John 16:28–33 in your Bible.
Next, complete the chart below, verse by verse.

Briefly write what each verse reveals to you about the Father, the Son, or the Holy Spirit. Perhaps the verse reflects a character trait of God (merciful, patient, gentle, loving). The verse might show what the Lord values (obedience, service) or how He wants us to behave (humbly, kindly, compassionately). It's fine to leave some spaces blank since you won't find an answer to the question in every verse. The idea is to read each verse thinking, *Does this verse tell me anything about God?* and then writing what comes to mind.

JOHN 16:28–33	What does this verse tell me about God?
28. "I came from the Father and have come into the world, and now I am leaving the world and going to the Father."	
29. His disciples said, "Ah, now you are speaking plainly and not using figurative speech!"	
30. "Now we know that you know all things and do not need anyone to question you; this is why we believe that you came from God."	

31. Jesus answered them,
"Do you now believe?"

32. "Behold, the hour is coming,
indeed it has come, when you
will be scattered, each to his
own home, and will leave me
alone. Yet I am not alone, for
the Father is with me."

33. "I have said these things to
you, that in me you may have
peace. In the world you will
have tribulation. But take heart;
I have overcome the world."

What strikes me first about today's verses is that once again we are reading that the disciples were having trouble believing that Jesus was from the Father. Finally, they "get it," and *now* they realized that Jesus knew all things and now they believed that He came from God.

Is it any wonder that people today struggle with understanding Jesus? Even the disciples didn't get it at first! Also, keep in mind that these verses make it clear that God alone grants understanding. Jesus told them He finally spoke plainly to them and they understood.

Read Matthew 13:34–35. Why did Jesus speak in parables?

Jesus was here to tell us things "hidden since the foundation of the world." By the time of His teachings in John 16:29, Jesus had stopped speaking in figures of speech, and spoke plainly.

Do you think these verses mean only that Jesus finally spoke in plain language and stopped using parables? Or do you think that what happened was that Jesus finally granted them understanding of things hidden since the foundation of the world? I think it is both, but I also think there was much they didn't understand until after the crucifixion and resurrection. Is there anything you are struggling to understand or believe in the Word right now? Write about it here:

Take a moment to pray now. Ask God to grant you the wisdom and discernment to understand His Word and His plan for you to serve Him.

The next part is a good example of the struggle we will face as believers. The disciples finally understood and believed. Then Jesus told them that they would be scattered and leave Him alone! Your faith will not shield you from the troubles of this world. In fact, "you will have tribulation" (John 16:33). What is your most troublesome "tribulation" right now?

As you face your tribulations, consider that Jesus knew that His disciples would scatter. Read Matthew 26:31. Notice that Jesus was telling the disciples that they would scatter and fulfill an Old Testament prophecy foretold in Zechariah 13:7: "Strike the shepherd, and the sheep will be scattered . . ." Keep in mind that God is in control. While you may not understand why you are facing this trouble, He does and He will use it for His glory. You can trust Him because, as seen throughout the Old and the New Testaments, God keeps His promises.

Read verse 32 again. Why do you think Jesus told the disciples that He would not be alone because the Father was with Him? On your first read, it may seem like Jesus was trying to alleviate any worry about Him. I think it has a different purpose. I think Jesus was giving us a concrete truth. Think about what He said over and over again during this final conversation with His disciples: through our faith in Him, we have a relationship with Him in all His fullness. If Jesus was not alone because the Father was with Him, then we are never without Him or the Father! Jesus was telling us that when we face trouble, we are not alone.

If Jesus were to show up in your home and tell you that He was there to help you get through the trouble you wrote about above, how would you feel about the trouble? Do you think your trouble would seem so "big" with Jesus sitting at your kitchen table? Would you worry about what you wrote above if you knew that Jesus was holding your hand as you dealt with your trouble? If Jesus *were* sitting at your kitchen table, what would you ask Him about the trouble you are dealing with right now? How would you ask Him to help you?

If you can't imagine Jesus sitting in your kitchen, how can you truly believe that He is always with you? Spend some time thinking about whether you *truly* believe in the promises we have been studying. Do you trust them in your heart and mind? If you do, you are so blessed! Spend time praising God for this amazing revelation. If you are struggling with this truth, you are not alone. Spend time rereading John 13–15. Pray for God to grant you understanding so that not only can you picture God dwelling within, you can *know* the certainty of Him working within you through the Holy Spirit.

You are not alone. You are never alone. Especially in times of trouble, God is with you—see Psalm 46:1. Read John 16:33 again and take in the beautiful love and magnificent power of our God. Jesus spoke these things so that in Him we would have peace. In the world we will have tribulation, but in Him we will have peace. What a glorious and loving God we serve! He gave us His Word so we can have peace. The world will give us trouble, but His Word will give us peace.

This is so true for me. When I spend time in prayer and in the Word, I have so much more peace in my day. I notice a remarkable difference if I do not make time for God and the Bible before I start my day. I do not feel centered. I feel frazzled and impatient. Have you ever experienced the difference? If you think about it, can you trace it back to spending time in His presence? Write what can happen when you do not spend time with God:

If you struggle to make time for your Bible, consider writing, "I have said these things to you, that in me you may have peace" somewhere you will see this verse as you begin your morning. Perhaps it will motivate you to slow down and start your day in God's Word.

Granting us peace demonstrates God's amazing love for us, but the next part speaks of His power: "Take heart; I have overcome the world" (John 16:33). This verse almost vibrates off the page when I read it. The power and might of our God is so awesome that we often cannot comprehend it. For some reason, this verse always makes me feel like God is protecting me—standing tall, feet planted, hands fisted, face overtaken with a fierceness that is terrifying. He is facing my attacker and protecting me with a Father's love.

After I shake in my boots at His power, I usually get tears in my eyes that He would fight for me. Next, I usually stand a little taller myself! The Creator of heaven and earth is my fierce protector. He has overcome the world. He has overcome evil. He has saved me from the world. Psalm 139 promises that He hems me in from behind and before. He is standing in front of me and promising me eternal life with Him in His kingdom!

Can you see Jesus fighting for you? Can you "take courage" and face what is troubling you when you picture Jesus standing in front of you, your strong protector, and standing behind you, your rear guard? What could you handle differently knowing that Jesus overcame it all? How could you change your attitude, thoughts, or behavior toward your trouble? How could you demonstrate your courage in Jesus? Write at least one way you could take courage in Jesus:

Reread John 14:27: "Peace I leave with you; my peace I give to you. Not as the world gives do I give to you. Let not your hearts be troubled, neither let them be afraid." Read Revelation 3:21, and write the promise God made to you:

Take courage! You can overcome anything through Christ.

> In all these things we are more than conquerors through him who loved us. —Romans 8:37

Closing Prayer: Father God, help me remember that Your love allows me to overwhelmingly conquer the troubles I face in this world. Lord, allow me to rest in Your power and Your peace. Let me take courage in Your power. Let me rest in Your peace today. Father, I want to set an example of courage in You. I want others to know that You have overcome the world! Grant me the revelations I need to serve You better. Grant me the understanding to grasp the amazing truth that You live within me and that I am never alone because I am always with You. Thank You, Lord, for Your love and Your magnificent power and protection. In Jesus' name I pray. Amen.

REVIEW, REFLECT, AND PRAY

Before you begin today, ask God to reveal anything you may have missed the first time through the lessons. Take time to review the verses for each day and fill in any spaces you left blank, if you can. Remember that it's the Lord through the Holy Spirit who grants understanding, especially when it comes to His Word. It's okay if you have empty spaces.

Read what you wrote about God in each chart and write your thoughts here:

Next, read what you wrote in response to the questions in the lessons and take a few minutes to pray.

If God revealed something to you this week, write about it here:

If God reminded you of something you've been forgetting lately, or showed you something that hasn't been part of your life for a while, write about it here:

If God challenged you this week to make a change in your life, how did He do it and what change will you make?

Before you end this week, take a few moments to be quiet and still. Take time to let the lessons of this week become wisdom in your heart. Take time to ask for His power and His peace!

> But thanks be to God, who in Christ always leads us in triumphal procession, and through us spreads the fragrance of the knowledge of him everywhere. —2 Corinthians 2:14

Closing Prayer: Father, thank You for Your Holy Spirit. I pray that the Holy Spirit will guide me into all truth and will remind me of the things I learned this week. Help me understand that my faith in Jesus makes me a child of God and that You are working through the Holy Spirit to change me. I want my life to be changed because of the overflow of the Holy Spirit so I may lead others to You. I ask, in the name of Jesus, for Your will to be done in my life and for my life to glorify You. I pray for courage to overcome this world. In Jesus' precious name I pray. Amen.

FILLED WITH THE HOLY SPIRIT

1. Review the lessons and what you wrote for Day 5. Share insights with the group.

2. Did you notice the pattern in John 16:8–11: Holy Spirit is God, Jesus is God, Father is God; the enemy, "the ruler of this world," is *not* any part of God and will be judged. What does this truth mean for you?

3. What impact did spending time thinking through John 16:13–15 have on you? Was it worthwhile to journal about these three verses? Why or why not?

4. Joy is a repeated theme in these chapters. John 16:22 says that no one will take your joy from you. Have these verses regarding joy spoken to you in any way?

5. Do you have any remaining questions about Jesus and whether He came forth from the Father and returned to heaven? or questions about the indwelling of the Holy Spirit?

6. Can you picture Jesus sitting at your kitchen table? What would you talk about?

7. If you need courage for something, please write it on the prayer requests this week. Call on Jesus to be your protector and provider!

8. Gather prayer requests for the week and close in prayer.

His final prayer

JOHN 17

We have a purple candy dish from my husband's grandmother, a hand-blown glass platter from my grandmother, a wooden turtle and some clay hippos that my in-laws picked up on trips—all placed lovingly around our home.

I smile as I dust these gifts and settle them carefully back in their spot. Sometimes when I see these things, memories founded in love come flooding to my mind. Each piece comes with its own special qualities and memories. I plan to someday pass these items on to my son. I hope that every time he sees them, he will be reminded he is loved.

Do you have any family heirlooms? Perhaps you have a gift given to you by your mother or father that you put in a special place. We treasure these types of gifts. When we receive a precious gift, given to us in love, it is significant.

Do you know that *you* are a precious gift from the Father to His Son, given in the purest, most amazing love? In Jesus' prayer in John 17, He acknowledged that the Father chose to call His children out of the world and give us to the Son. We were chosen by the Father as a precious gift to the Son! I remember when I first understood what Jesus was praying in this chapter 17. I was a brand-new believer, beginning my Bible reading in the book of John. When I first encountered Jesus' prayer, I had to read it several times because it seemed too good to be true. I heard the Lord whisper into my heart, "You are mine and you are a precious gift." To my knees I went, tears streaming down my face.

I always knew that I was loved by my family. But they are my parents and siblings—they have to love me! I don't want you to misunderstand and think that I don't treasure the love of my family, because I do. It's just that I was raised to believe that it's a given that family members love each other and stick together. To think I could be considered a precious gift for Christ from the God of the universe . . . now that is something! It overwhelmed me, humbled me, and healed me. If the God of heaven and earth drew me to Him, then maybe, just maybe, I *could* live this life described in the Bible. Jesus' prayer made me *want* to live my life differently so I might be able to bring honor to being a chosen and treasured gift.

> **As you study this final prayer of Jesus,
> see how many times "love" appears.**

John 17 is the only lengthy prayer of Jesus recorded in the Bible. The New Testament has several references to Jesus praying to His Father, but only chapter 17 in the book of John reflects a more complete prayer. This prayer is an outpouring of the heart of Jesus to His Father in prayer. The heart of Jesus and the Father are evident in every line. I pray that you will give yourself some extra time this week to sit in wonder as you work through this holy conversation.

Many women I know immediately think, "How could *I* be worthy of belonging to Him?" We women often tend to undervalue our talents and gifts. Well, it's tough to argue with the Creator of the universe. He considers you a precious gift! As you work through the lessons, you will see that everything Jesus prayed circles back to the "why." Pay special attention to the verses that say "so that" the world may know or believe. In this prayer, Jesus revealed the purpose of every Christian life—to love others *so that* the world will know Jesus. As you study this final prayer of Jesus, see how many times "love" appears. The heart of Jesus is beautifully captured and revealed to us in this chapter of our study. I pray that it will change your life as it did mine. You are a precious gift!

WEEK 5 | DAY 1

GLORIFY THE FATHER

Read John 17:1–8 in your Bible.
Then fill in the chart, verse by verse.

Briefly write what each verse reveals to you about the Father, the Son, or the Holy Spirit. Perhaps the verse reflects a character trait of God (merciful, patient, gentle, loving). The verse might show what the Lord values (obedience, service) or how He wants us to behave (humbly, kindly, compassionately). It's fine to leave some spaces blank since you won't find an answer to the question in every verse. The idea is to read each verse thinking, *Does this verse tell me anything about God?* and then writing what comes to mind.

JOHN 17:1–8	What does this verse tell me about God?
1. When Jesus had spoken these words, he lifted up his eyes to heaven, and said, "Father, the hour has come; glorify your Son that the Son may glorify you,"	
2. "since you have given him authority over all flesh, to give eternal life to all whom you have given him."	
3. "And this is eternal life, that they know you the only true God, and Jesus Christ whom you have sent."	

4. "I glorified you on earth, having accomplished the work that you gave me to do."

5. "And now, Father, glorify me in your own presence with the glory that I had with you before the world existed."

6. "I have manifested your name to the people whom you gave me out of the world. Yours they were, and you gave them to me, and they have kept your word."

7. "Now they know that everything that you have given me is from you."

8. "For I have given them the words that you gave me, and they have received them and have come to know in truth that I came from you; and they have believed that you sent me."

Do you still wonder if heaven is real? Heaven is referenced in Scripture on several occasions. Notice that verse 1 says, Jesus "lifted up his eyes to heaven." Heaven is certainly a real place! Take a moment and look at the amazing sky or stars. Imagine a place so amazing and pure that mere words cannot describe it. Take a moment and imagine seeing Jesus face-to-face. Oh glorious day!

God gave Jesus authority over all flesh so that Jesus could grant eternal life to all those who had been given to Him. Once again we see that God is responsible for calling people to Jesus and salvation. Notice how this is written: to all whom are given to Him, He may grant eternal life. *Nothing* we have—even our salvation—would have been granted to us but for God's will. For God's glory, the Son will grant eternal life to those given to Him by the Father. How do you react to belonging to the Creator of the universe? Is this a difficult concept for you to accept? Why?

Jesus told the Jews:

> ". . . but you do not believe because you are not among my sheep. My sheep hear my voice, and I know them, and they follow me. I give them eternal life, and they will never perish, and no one will snatch them out of my hand. My Father, who has given them to me, is greater than all, and no one is able to snatch them out of the Father's hand. I and the Father are one." (John 10:26–30)

Some will not believe because they refuse to hear His voice. But those who do hear His voice are His forever, and nothing can change that fact. Nothing can separate you from your Father in heaven.

How many times in chapter 17 did Jesus tell the disciples that we were given to Him by the Father? At least four times; review verses 2, 6, 9, and 24. Now read John 6:39: "This is the will of him who sent me, that I should lose nothing of all that he has given me, but raise it up on the last day." The Lord does not want to lose anyone. Everything has been given into His hands, and it is the will of the

Father that no one would be lost.

Read Luke 13:22–27. How did Jesus respond to the question about whether only a few would be saved? Notice how the people tried to "enter through the narrow door" by claiming that they ate and drank in His presence and that He taught in their streets. Do you see the point Jesus is making? Jesus is the narrow door. Remember that Jesus told us that no one comes to the Father except through Him. Jesus is the way (John 14:6).

Just believing that Jesus existed on this planet is not enough. You must develop a relationship with Him. In verse 3, Jesus told us that eternal life is to *know* the only true God and Jesus Christ. Do you *know* the only true God? Do you *know* Jesus Christ? How would you describe your relationship with the Lord right now?

Jesus said, "Not everyone who says to Me, 'Lord, Lord,' will enter the kingdom of heaven, but the one who does the will of my Father who is in heaven. On that day many will say to me, 'Lord, Lord, did we not prophesy in your name, and cast out demons in your name, and do many mighty works in your name?' And then will I declare to them, 'I never knew you; depart from me, you workers of lawlessness'" (Matthew 7:21–23).

It is not enough to have head knowledge of the Lord. You must be one "who does the will of my Father." How do you know the will of the Father? What steps are you taking to seek the will of the Father? Are you spending time in prayer and in His Word?

Jesus also warned the Jews not to seek glory from one another, but rather to seek the glory of God. "How can you believe, when you receive glory from one another and do not seek the glory that comes from the only God?" (John 5:44). Are you seeking God's glory?

What do you do on a regular basis to try to *know* the Father, to hear His will, to seek His glory?

When we get busy, it is easy to believe that we do not have time to talk and listen to God, but we need to ask ourselves this: Is anything I have to do today more important than hearing God say, "I know you"? Before we put off our prayer time or Bible study, let's ask ourselves if those items on our to-do list are worth hearing the Lord say, "I never knew you. Depart from me." I want to ask myself if those things I *must* do today (instead of spending time with God) are seeking God's glory or are those things I will do to seek glory from others. Take some time to reflect and pray about these questions and your answers. Please understand that the Lord is not judging you with regard to the time you spend in prayer or reading your Bible. It is not a box to be checked or a set requirement for salvation. But the Lord does want a relationship with you. He wants you to know Him.

Next, Jesus said that He glorified God by accomplishing the work He was given to do on earth. In Matthew 7:21–23 (above), Jesus said that those who *do* the will of the Lord will enter the kingdom of heaven. How many times in the previous chapters did Jesus tell us to obey His commandments? In these final hours, Jesus told the disciples many, many times that to love Him is to obey Him. In other words, we *do* the will of the Father because we know Him and love Him. Accomplish the work He has given us to do on this earth so that our lives glorify the Lord.

What work has the Lord given you to accomplish?

When the disciples found Jesus talking to the Samaritan woman at the well, they urged Him to eat. Jesus responded, "My food is to do the will of him who sent me and to accomplish his work" (John 4:34). Are you *that* focused on what the Lord is asking you to do? Are you doing it to the glory of God?

Jesus next acknowledged, once again, that the disciples were given to Him "out of the world. Yours they were, and you gave them to me, and they have kept your word" (John 17:6). Jesus also expressed the disciples' faith and sincere belief that Jesus came from the Father. He said they received the message and now "know in truth" that Jesus came from God and was sent by God. Do you truly understand that Jesus came from God and was sent by God? Do you remember when you first realized this truth?

Take a moment to pray about whatever you wrote—either in thanksgiving for God's divine wisdom and understanding of His truth—or request that God grant you understanding through the Holy Spirit. Ask God to remove your doubts and answer your questions. Be still and allow the Holy Spirit to speak into your heart.

I remember when I was skeptical about Jesus. Sure, I believed He walked the earth and was probably an amazing person, but I didn't really believe with all my heart that He was God. I just couldn't wrap my head around it. How could God be in heaven *and* on earth at the same time? I also didn't understand how a loving God could reject so many people and send them to hell for eternity, no matter how "good" a person was on earth. Jesus as the *only* way to heaven seemed too harsh to be true. I just couldn't picture heaven as a real place where some people go, but others would be excluded.

But on the morning of April 25, 2008, as Austin was leaving this world, God allowed me to have a glimpse of heaven in my heart. The impression was beyond words. I had just received a call that an ambulance was at our house and the paramedics were working on Austin. On the drive from work to the hospital, in my heart, I was begging Austin to fight and to stay with mommy. "But Mom," Austin's voice rang in my heart, "it's so pretty here . . ." I could feel that he wanted to stay and what I felt was too wonderful to be anything other than heaven itself. I let Austin go in that moment. "Okay, angel," I said, "okay." And just like that, Austin went to heaven. The feeling ended as quickly as it appeared, but I was no longer skeptical about heaven.

With certainty in my heart about heaven, I began my search for what else was true about God, Jesus, and the Bible. My salvation story is like a toddler's leap off the edge of a pool into a father's arms. Knowing heaven was real, I just jumped into my faith. I accepted Jesus as my Lord and Savior because I knew heaven was real and I wanted to go there with Austin. I learned to "swim" with the help of the Holy Spirit. Each day as I read my Bible, the Holy Spirit whispered instructions and insights.

Reading my Bible (especially studying these chapters in John's gospel) and seeking understanding through the Holy Spirit led me out of skepticism and into trust for God's loving sovereignty. I cannot claim to fully understand why some will go to heaven and others will spend eternity in hell. I do understand that salvation and eternal life in heaven involves one simple act—making Jesus the Lord and Savior of your life. Accepting the gift of Jesus' death on the cross in exchange for your life means that you will go to heaven.

If we think about salvation as a gift, it seems to make more sense to our human mind. If someone offers you a gift, and you reject it and leave it sitting unopened on the table, you don't get the benefit or the joy of the gift. It just sits there. It also stands as a rejection of the person giving the gift. Rejecting a gift is an insult in any culture.

Salvation is a gift. God offers the gift of eternal life in heaven through faith in Jesus as His one and only Son. The gift of salvation is open to every person. The reality is, however, that some will reject the gift. Those who accept the gift from the Father acknowledge and accept His role as Lord of their life. As a result, heaven's gates swing joyfully open. I pray that your study of these final words of Jesus eliminates any remaining skepticism about God's love for you and the certainty of your salvation.

If you haven't accepted the gift of Jesus yet, I hope you take that leap of faith into your Father's loving arms today. If you haven't truly made Jesus Lord and Savior in your life, I encourage you to pray this prayer of commitment to Him:

> *Father God, I know that I need a Savior. I need forgiveness for my sins. I believe that Jesus is Your one and only begotten Son, that He died on the cross to take the judgment for my sins, and that He rose from the dead and now sits with You in heaven. Jesus, I ask You to come into my life and allow the Holy Spirit to change my heart. Forgive my sins. Make me a new person. Jesus, I make You my Lord and Savior. In Jesus' name I pray. Amen.*

You did it! You jumped and your heavenly Father now has you wrapped tightly in His arms. Your life will never be the same. Welcome to the family, child of God. (I wish I could hug you in person right now!) I encourage you to tell someone else that you have put your trust in Jesus Christ as your Savior. Reach out to your Bible study teacher, pastor's wife, or another Christian friend so they can journey with you in your new relationship with Christ.

"I am the good shepherd. I know my own and my own know me, just as the Father knows me and I know the Father; and I lay down my life for the sheep." —John 10:14–15

Closing Prayer: Oh Father, my prayer is that I might know You! Allow the Holy Spirit to speak truth to my heart and help me to truly understand that Jesus came forth from God and was sent by God. I pray that I will comprehend that I am not a part of this world's system and that I now sit in Your mighty hand. Lord, I am so thankful that nothing can snatch me from Your hand. It is my desire to seek You, to know You, to know Your will, and to accomplish the work You have given me to do on this earth. Lord, give me the courage and the strength to do Your will and to glorify You by doing it well. In Jesus' name I pray. Amen.

WEEK 5 | DAY 2

NOT OF THIS WORLD

Read John 17:9–16 in your Bible.
Next, complete the chart below, verse by verse.

Briefly write what each verse reveals to you about the Father, the Son, or the Holy Spirit. Perhaps the verse reflects a character trait of God (merciful, patient, gentle, loving). The verse might show what the Lord values (obedience, service) or how He wants us to behave (humbly, kindly, compassionately). It's fine to leave some spaces blank since you won't find an answer to the question in every verse. The idea is to read each verse thinking, *Does this verse tell me anything about God?* and then writing what comes to mind.

John 17:9–16	What does this verse tell me about God?
9. "I am praying for them. I am not praying for the world but for those whom you have given me, for they are yours."	
10. "All mine are yours, and yours are mine, and I am glorified in them."	
11. "And I am no longer in the world, but they are in the world, and I am coming to you. Holy Father, keep them in your name, which you have given me, that they may be one, even as we are one."	

12. "While I was with them, I kept them in your name, which you have given me. I have guarded them, and not one of them has been lost except the son of destruction, that the Scripture might be fulfilled."

13. "But now I am coming to you, and these things I speak in the world, that they may have my joy fulfilled in themselves."

14. "I have given them your word, and the world has hated them because they are not of the world, just as I am not of the world."

15. "I do not ask that you take them out of the world, but that you keep them from the evil one."

16. "They are not of the world, just as I am not of the world."

Today's passage reminds me of the Carrie Underwood song "Temporary Home," because these verses and that song tell us that we do not belong here. We do not belong on this earth, in this world, in this culture. We have a purpose for being here, but this fallen earth is not our home. Our place is with our Creator. Throughout today's verses, Jesus made it clear that the world was separate from Him.

Jesus said He was not praying to the Father on behalf of the world, but rather for those who believe in Him, for those who were given to Him by the Father. Jesus asked the Father to keep the disciples in the Father's name, in the name of Jesus, and to make them one, even as He is one with the Father. Write Jesus' petition in verses 9–11 in your own words:

Jesus explained that while He was with the disciples, He "kept them" and He "guarded them." Remember my mental picture of the Lord standing, feet planted, hands fisted, face fierce, standing in front of us as our protector? Jesus clearly told the disciples that He *is* their protector. He asked the Father to protect the disciples from evil as He went to the cross.

If you could ask the Lord to stand in front of you right now as your protector, what evil would you ask Him to protect you from in your life? How could the Lord protect you right now?

In verse 13, Jesus explained that He came to the world and spoke these words so that you might have *His* joy "made full" in yourself. Look back at Week 4, Day 3 (page 128) and consider again the things you wrote that were stealing your joy and whether those things had any eternal significance. How are you doing with those items? Are you letting them get to you? Write about your progress or roadblocks to living a joy-filled life:

Can we truly comprehend all the truths in the passage today? Seriously—it's remarkable stuff. Let me summarize for you: We are not of this world. As followers of the Creator of the universe, we live apart from the system of this world. Jesus came to speak these truths so that we could live a life filled with divine joy—so that we could be "made full" of His joy. It is beyond comprehension. It is likely your brain cannot process this information logically. You must do it in faith. You must simply trust in the Word of God and listen to the small, still voice within that calls you toward God.

Take a few minutes to let these truths sink into your mind. Let these truths become wisdom within. Journal your response to these truths or write what the Holy Spirit is speaking to you today as you reflect on the Lord's awesome love for you.

We have been picturing the Lord as our fierce protector and imagining Him standing in front of us, so I do not want you to miss the powerful statement in verse 15: "I do not ask that you take them out of the world, but that you keep them from the evil one."

Jesus specifically asked God to protect His followers from the evil one. During his time on earth, Jesus dealt with Satan directly for forty days in the desert (Matthew 4:1–11). He cast out demons and evil spirits. Scripture states these circumstances as matter of fact, not as fiction or cases of mental disturbance. The reality of the enemy and spiritual warfare are many times dealt with in Scripture. Yet in today's world, speaking of Satan as if he really exists can be viewed as weird. Even some Christians seem to hesitate to discuss the reality of Satan openly, and his existence and influence is often mocked by entertainers. But Peter warned: "Be sober-minded; be watchful. Your adversary the devil prowls around like a roaring lion, seeking someone to devour" (1 Peter 5:8).

What are these passages, John 17:15 and 1 Peter 5:8, telling us?

Jesus spoke specifically about the "evil one." Do you think He was making up a scary story? Do you think He was exaggerating to frighten us into obedience to Him? No? Then you must admit that the "evil one" exists *and* that he is a threat to us. Otherwise, why was Jesus praying about the "evil one" in His final hours?

Perhaps our adversary no longer needs to prowl around; since our culture has relegated him to the world of fiction, he just walks among us unnoticed! But as Ephesians 6:12 reminds us, our struggle is not with forces of flesh and blood, but with unseen "spiritual forces of evil." The Christian term for this certainty is *spiritual warfare*.

Satan is as real as anything we can see or touch. But how often do we intentionally try to protect against him? How often do we warn our children of him? These days, our kids are never out of our sight, they get a multitude of vaccines, they stay in car seats until they are practically teenagers, and yet most of us do not speak openly and honestly to our children about the devil. It is difficult and frightening. It's not pleasant. But we must do it!

Ephesians 6:10–18 is a well-known passage about fighting these spiritual forces. In addition, we should avail ourselves of Christian books and resources that address this reality from a biblical viewpoint. Some ideas are listed in the Notes section of this book.[7]

Is there anyone in your life who would benefit from understanding that spiritual warfare exists? If yes, write who it is and write a short prayer to God for their understanding and protection. You might even use the words of Ephesians 6 as you pray.

As I've mentioned, 1 Peter 5:8 tells us to "be sober-minded; be watchful. Your adversary the devil prowls around like a roaring lion, seeking someone to devour." We're then told in 1 Peter 5:9–11 to "resist him, firm in your faith, knowing that the same kinds of suffering are being experienced by your brotherhood throughout the world. And after you have suffered a little while, the God of all grace, who has called you to his eternal glory in Christ, will himself restore, confirm, strengthen, and establish you. To him be the dominion forever and ever. Amen."

Take a deep breath and step out in faith. If Jesus acknowledged the evil one, so must we. We cannot fight him together if we do not talk to each other about him and stand in victory together. Our silence or apathy is one of the enemy's greatest victories. All the better to prowl around and devour us! Remember that 1 John 4:4 promises, "he who is in you is greater than he who is in the world."

If you have experienced spiritual warfare, or have faced the enemy in your own life, write some examples here and share them with your group:

In Luke 22:31–32, Jesus told Peter, "Simon, Simon, behold, Satan demanded to have you, that he might sift you like wheat, but I have prayed for you that your faith may not fail." Keep in mind, even in spiritual warfare, God is in control and prayer works to protect us. The enemy is not going to like our speaking about him like this one little bit. So take a moment to pray for the Lord's protection from the evil one as we expose his darkness. Take a moment to pray for the protection of the leaders of this study and the other women in your group.

> Put on the whole armor of God, that you may be able to stand against the schemes of the devil. —Ephesians 6:11

Closing Prayer: Father, we need Your protection from the evil one. Help us put on the full armor of Your protection by spending time in prayer and in Your Word. Lord, it is my prayer that I would live in this world as an example of Your love. Since You have brought me out of this world and its ways, please help me live in a way that separates me from this world. I want my everyday life to set an example of how a child of God is to live in this world until You call me home. Lord, I am so grateful that this is our temporary home, and that I will spend eternal life in Your kingdom. Prepare me for my permanent home, Father, and protect me while I work to fulfill Your plan for me in this one. In Jesus' name I pray. Amen.

SANCTIFIED!

Read John 17:17–20 in your Bible.
Then fill in the chart, verse by verse.

Briefly write what each verse reveals to you about the Father, the Son, or the Holy Spirit. Perhaps the verse reflects a character trait of God (merciful, patient, gentle, loving). The verse might show what the Lord values (obedience, service) or how He wants us to behave (humbly, kindly, compassionately). It's fine to leave some spaces blank since you won't find an answer to the question in every verse. The idea is to read each verse thinking, *Does this verse tell me anything about God?* and then writing what comes to mind.

JOHN 17:17–20	What does this verse tell me about God?
17. "Sanctify them in the truth; your word is truth."	
18. "As you sent me into the world, so I have sent them into the world."	
19. "And for their sake I consecrate myself, that they also may be sanctified in truth."	
20. "I do not ask for these only, but also for those who will believe in me through their word,"	

Okay–I'll admit it. I had to look up "sanctify" to see exactly what it meant. What a marvelous thing! The concordance in my study Bible says sanctify means "set apart to God." Reread the verses above and replace sanctify with "set apart to God." Jesus prayed for you to be set apart to God. Read carefully and see that Jesus prayed for you to be set apart to God, in truth, in Jesus. Remember that Jesus is the way, *the truth*, and the life. Doesn't this just make you shake your head in humble disbelief?

Write your reaction to being "set apart to God."

Jesus sent the disciples (and us) into the world. Write about the last time you shared the gospel with someone.

Verse 20 is special to me. I remember the first time I read it. I went back and reread it because this verse told me that Jesus' whole prayer applied not only to the disciples who lived with Him more than two thousand years ago, but His prayer also was meant for me. It made me feel like Jesus was expecting me, that He knew me, that He had plans for me, and that He prayed for *me*! We pray for those we love. Verse 20 makes me feel loved by Jesus—a personal, heartfelt prayer for me in His final hours. It nearly makes me weep.

Have you ever read this passage before? Maybe you're noticing this key verse for the first time. Have you ever really thought about this prayer before? Have you ever taken a moment to think about who you would pray for in your final hours? What would you pray for your loved ones if you had one last prayer? Have you ever realized that Jesus prayed for *you* in His final hours?

Reread all of chapter 17 out loud and insert your name in it. Read it aloud as a **prayer for you personally.** Write what the Holy Spirit speaks into your heart as you listen to Jesus' prayer for *you.*

Consider what you must mean to the Lord for Him to pray for you in His final hours. Consider that He would set you apart to Him. Take a moment and reflect on being a child of God.

> Little children, you are from God and have overcome them, for he who is in you is greater than he who is in the world. —1 John 4:4

Closing Prayer: Father, I am in awe of You. All the glory, honor, and praise go to You. I pray that I will live every day as someone who is set apart to God. My desire is to be sanctified in Your truth. Lord, let Your truth become part of me. Let Your love overflow into the world through me. Father, help me always remember that I am a child of God and important to You. Help me remember that prayer is powerful and that You prayed for *me*! Help me remember that You sent us into the world to spread Your truth so others could know You. I pray that the Holy Spirit would draw me to someone who needs to hear the gospel and that I will be bold enough to declare Your amazing love! In Jesus' name I pray. Amen.

WEEK 5 | DAY 4

HIS FINAL PRAYER

Read John 17:21–26 in your Bible.
Next, complete the chart below, verse by verse.

Briefly write what each verse reveals to you about the Father, the Son, or the Holy Spirit. Perhaps the verse reflects a character trait of God (merciful, patient, gentle, loving). The verse might show what the Lord values (obedience, service) or how He wants us to behave (humbly, kindly, compassionately). It's fine to leave some spaces blank since you won't find an answer to the question in every verse. The idea is to read each verse thinking, *Does this verse tell me anything about God?* and then writing what comes to mind.

JOHN 17:21–26	What does this verse tell me about God?
21. "that they may all be one, just as you, Father, are in me, and I in you, that they also may be in us, so that the world may believe that you have sent me."	
22. "The glory that you have given me I have given to them, that they may be one even as we are one,"	
23. "I in them and you in me, that they may become perfectly one, so that the world may know that you sent me and loved them even as you loved me."	

24. "Father, I desire that they also, whom you have given me, may be with me where I am, to see my glory that you have given me because you loved me before the foundation of the world."

25. "O righteous Father, even though the world does not know you, I know you, and these know that you have sent me."

26. "I made known to them your name, and I will continue to make it known, that the love with which you have loved me may be in them, and I in them."

Do you see what Jesus prayed for you? He prayed that we (believers) may all be one, and that you may be "in" the Father and the Son (v. 21). Jesus prayed that, through His glory, we may be one, just as the Father and the Son are one (v. 22). He prayed that believers would be perfected in unity with Him and the Father (v. 23). Jesus asked that we would be with Him where He is (in heaven) and see His glory (v. 24).

Look closely and see *why* Jesus asked the Father for these things. Reread today's passage and note where it says, "so that" in verses 21 and 23. What was Jesus' prayer in these verses?

What was Jesus' purpose in His prayer in verses 24 and 26?

Write *why* you think Jesus prayed the way He did in His final hours:

Can you see that Jesus' prayer is about spreading the gospel and giving glory to God? Jesus came to this world *so that* you might be saved and become a child of God. Jesus came *so that* you might be with Him in heaven, and *so that* you would experience God's love. Last, but certainly not least, Jesus came and died on the cross *so that* you would show the world His love, and *so that* others might believe that Jesus was from the Father—that Jesus was who He said He was—the Messiah.

Read Galatians 3:26–29 and write what you think these verses mean in light of Jesus' prayer:

How do you feel about Jesus' prayer now? Though our salvation does not depend on works (see Ephesians 2:8–9), our faith does result in action (see James 2:17, 26). How are you fulfilling Jesus' prayer for unity among believers so the world will be pointed to Christ? Be as specific as you can.

In Romans 12:5–6, Paul wrote, "so we, though many, are one body in Christ, and individually members one of another. Having gifts that differ according to the grace given to us, let us use them . . . in proportion to our faith." What are your gifts? Write at least one of your strengths below and explain how you could use this gift to serve God's kingdom and His purpose.

Before we close today, reread the last verse of our study: "I made known to them your name, and I will continue to make it known, that the love with which you have loved me may be in them, and I in them." Praise Jesus! Jesus came so that you might have God's love in you and so that you might have Jesus in you. He came because you are loved. You are deeply and divinely loved. The Creator of the universe wants you to have His love in you. Do you have a big smile on your face right now? Do you have a warm feeling in your heart right now thinking about it? Good! Now what are you going to do with it?

How are you going to fulfill God's purpose so that the world will also know what you know about Him? How will your "light shine before others, so that they may see your good works and give glory to your Father who is in heaven" (Matthew 5:16)? What are you going to do to live a life that reflects how much God loves us? Try spending just five minutes thinking about God's amazing love for you and how you might spread that love around you. Seriously, look at the clock and give yourself five minutes to brainstorm what you could do to honor Jesus' prayer for you.

What came to mind? Write your ideas here:

For God so loved the world, that he gave his only Son, that whoever believes in him should not perish but have eternal life. For God did not send his Son into the world to condemn the world, but in order that the world might be saved through him. —John 3:16–17

Closing Prayer: Father, my prayer is that I would show others Your love. I pray that people around me would be drawn to Jesus partly because of my actions. Lord, help me recognize the unique gifts You have given me so I may serve not only my brothers and sisters in Christ, but also "the least of these" in this world. I am in awe of Your divine love for me and for this world. I am humbled that You would love me and want Your love to reside in me and through me. Lord, I want to honor Your beautiful prayer by abiding in Your love so that the world may believe in You. In Jesus' name I pray. Amen.

WEEK 5 | DAY 5

REVIEW, REFLECT, AND PRAY

Before you begin today, ask God to reveal anything you may have missed the first time through the lessons. Take time to review the verses for each day and fill in any spaces you left blank, if you can. Remember that only God through the Holy Spirit grants understanding, especially when it comes to His Word. It's okay if you have empty spaces.

Read what you wrote about God in each chart and write your thoughts here:

Next, read what you wrote in response to the questions in the lessons and take a few minutes to pray.

If God revealed something to you this week, write about it here:

If God reminded you of something you've been forgetting lately, or showed you something that hasn't been part of your life for a while, write about it here:

If God challenged you to make a change in your life, how did He do it and what change will you make?

Before you end this week, take a few moments to be quiet and still. Take time to let the lessons of this week become wisdom in your heart. Think about how you can reflect His amazing love to others!

"As the Father has loved me, so have I loved you. Abide in my love."
—John 15:9

Closing Prayer: Father, as I reflect on Jesus' prayer, my desire is to honor You in every way. I pray that my thoughts, words, and actions will show that I am set apart in You. Thank You for choosing me! I pray that I will be courageous and bold in sharing the gospel. Lord, I pray that Your joy will be made full in me so that others will see Your divine love and joy in my life. My prayer is that I will use my gifts as You intended: to serve Your kingdom and honor Your purpose. I pray that my life gives You glory, honor, and praise. In Jesus' name I pray. Amen.

DISCUSSION GUIDE | WEEK FIVE: JOHN 17

HIS FINAL PRAYER

1. Review the lessons and what you wrote for Day 5. Share insights with the group.

2. Did the Scripture where Jesus said, "And then will I declare to them, 'I never knew you; depart from me, you workers of lawlessness'" have an impact you?

3. Share your spiritual gifts with the group and discuss the steps you are taking to do the work God has given you to do. Ask for help or ideas where you are struggling to identify your gift or use your gift.

4. How does it make you feel to be His? How does it make you feel to belong to the Creator of all things, the almighty, all-powerful God?

5. How does it make you feel to be cherished by the Son? So cherished that He would teach you, die for you, share His kingdom with you, guard you, pray for you, and love you?

6. Do you have any spiritual warfare stories to share?

7. What could you do to honor Jesus' prayer for you?

8. Gather prayer requests for the week and close in prayer.

His final words

JOHN 18–21

After His time with the disciples was over, Jesus spoke very few words throughout His arrest, trial, and crucifixion. Don't let the number of His words fool you, however, because this last week of study is incredibly powerful! As you study the final words of Christ in John's gospel, chapters 18–21, you will see things come full circle.

In His final words, you will see that Jesus resolved, reconciled, restored, and renewed:

• **Resolved:** Jesus was absolutely resolved to follow the will of the Father. He willingly went to the cross to die for our sins because He was resolved to give glory to God and save us. Jesus was resolved to accomplish the work the Father had given Him, even to death.

• **Reconciled:** Jesus reconciled the Old Testament prophecies during His arrest, crucifixion, and resurrection. You will see Scripture fulfilled as Jesus completed His final days on earth. Jesus also reconciled our relationship with the Father by taking our place on the cross. The sacrifice of Jesus reconciled believers and God.

• **Restored:** Jesus restored His followers' faith when He rose from the dead. Jesus restored the joy of the women who served Him by first appearing to Mary Magdalene and sending her to be the first person to share the good news. The disciples' joy was restored when they saw Jesus in their midst after His death on the cross.

• **Renewed:** Jesus renewed the conviction and commitment of His disciples when He restored Peter's position as a leader among the disciples. When He blessed them with a great number of fish after His resurrection, Jesus renewed their conviction that He would provide for them and care for them as He sent them into the world. Jesus renewed the disciples' commitment by sending them in His place.

In these final words, Jesus again gave examples and instruction for being a Christ follower. He showed us how to walk it out in our lives. Jesus told us what is expected of us as believers. He reminded us who He is—"I am He." Jesus proved in these final chapters that He is the King of kings and the Lord of lords. I can't wait for us to sit in amazement at His glory! Let's dive in!

WEEK 6 | DAY 1

THE POWER OF HIS WORDS

Read John 18 in your Bible. I encourage you to read it out loud to cement the truths into your heart and mind.

In this final week of studying the last words of Christ, we begin with a reminder that the very breath of God is enough to shake the earth. We should never forget that God merely spoke our world into existence:

> In the beginning, God created the heavens and the earth. The earth was without form and void, and darkness was over the face of the deep. And the Spirit of God was hovering over the face of the waters.
>
> And God said, "Let there be light," and there was light.
> —Genesis 1:1–3

The very beginning of the Bible reveals how the Lord created the earth and all the things we see around us. Every single living thing, every star in the sky was spoken into life by God. As we turn to John 18, we see the power in the voice of God again. Jesus and the disciples left the upper room and walked to a garden near the Mount of Olives. Judas, along with the chief priests, Pharisees, and a group of Roman soldiers came to the garden of Gethsemane to arrest Jesus. Jesus asks them, "Whom do you seek?"

Write verse 6:

Can you imagine being bowled over by the breath of God? Can you imagine a large group of people falling to the ground all at once? All Jesus said was, "I am he." But if we remember that God spoke the world into existence, and recall that God told Abraham simply, "I am," the words "I am he" vibrate with power and authority.

Are you a bit surprised that the group had the nerve to answer Jesus again? After they stood back up and dusted themselves off, Jesus asks them again. Write verses 7 and 8:

Did you notice that our Savior, once again, put others first? He protected the disciples: "let these men go." Of course, Peter steps out again—he cuts off the ear of the high priest's servant (v. 10). Jesus, once again, rebukes Peter. Write verse 11b:

This reference to the "cup" that the Father had given Jesus to "drink" appears in all four Gospels (Matthew 26:39; Mark 14:36; Luke 22:42). In Matthew, Mark, and Luke, the reference to the "cup" also contains a request by Jesus to His Father to "let this cup pass from me" or "remove this cup from me," followed by His complete submission to the Father's will: "yet not what I will, but what you will." "Not my will, but yours, be done."

When I first encountered this scene in my Bible, I was in deep grief. Austin's room was still filled with his bed, toys, books . . . I could still see his fingerprints on his window. The pain in my heart was still incredibly sharp and very heavy. Yet I was a new believer, falling in love with Jesus. For the first time, I was beginning to comprehend what Jesus did for me. When I read how He agonized, praying in such agony that blood dripped from Him, I could relate to such agony. When He asked the Father to "remove this cup from me," I felt somehow relieved and understood. Jesus endured incredible grief and pain. Jesus knew what my heart felt like. And still, Jesus submitted His will to the Father's will.

After reading this scene in each gospel, I gained a deep understanding that we don't have to like what the Father sets before us (remove this cup from me), but we must bend our will to the Father's (yet, not my will, but Yours). Below, write about something that is difficult for you to accept:

Next, write Jesus' words back to His Father. Write "yet, not my will, but Yours" below and pray to be able to accept the path set before you, knowing that though you have asked God to remove a "cup" from you, you are prepared to continue in complete submission to His will for your life:

It may be helpful to remember that the apostle Paul had a "thorn in the flesh," which he asked God to remove. The Lord's reply was that "My grace is sufficient for you."

Jesus, our Savior, our Intercessor, our Protector, knows exactly how you feel. When bad things happen, try not to let your circumstances crowd out your faith in a Father who loves you. Trust that Jesus understands your suffering and is agonizing over your circumstances, too. The Father will use your circumstances to further His kingdom. A sweet mentor told me, "God holds every tear you cry. He won't waste a single tear." I pray that the Lord removes whatever you wrote above, but if He doesn't, I pray that a deep peace settles over your heart.

Knowing what was going to happen, knowing His time had come, Jesus went willingly. He was arrested, bound, and taken to the high priest of the Jews. Write how Jesus answered when questioned about His teaching (vv. 20 and 21):

One of the officers thought Jesus disrespected the high priest and struck Jesus. Jesus responded by saying, "If what I said is wrong, bear witness about the wrong; but if what I said is right, why do you strike me?"

These verses remind me that we will encounter people who will lash out at us for speaking the truth about Jesus. Jesus responded to the officer's lashing out by pointing back to the truth. Studying the Word of God will help us point others back to the truth.

After being questioned by the high priest, Jesus was taken to Pilate at the Praetorium. Pontius Pilate was the Roman governor over Judea, and the Praetorium was used as a temporary Roman military headquarters. First, Pilate questioned the Jews, asking what accusations were being brought against Jesus. Pilate tried to get the Jews to take responsibility for Jesus, but they wanted Him put to death but were not permitted by Jewish law to do so themselves (vv. 28–32).

Next, Pilate questions Jesus: "Are you the King of the Jews?" How does Jesus respond in verse 34?

What do you think Jesus was trying to accomplish by asking Pilate this question?

At first, I skimmed over this verse, thinking that Jesus was just questioning Pilate's information. However, considering how few words Jesus spoke after His arrest, I went back and pondered this question. I wonder if this question is posed to every single person on earth: Do you know that Jesus is King or did others tell you about Him? In other words, do *you* really know who Jesus is or is your faith based on what others have told you? Have *you* made the personal decision to make Jesus your Lord, or are you going along based on how you were raised? Similarly, do *you* know the Word of God or do you rely on others to tell you what the Bible says?

As I wrote in the beginning, it is my heartfelt prayer that this study has deepened your knowledge of Jesus and the Bible. I pray that this study of the last words of Christ has brought you personally closer to Jesus!

When Pilate responded by saying, "Am I a Jew?" Jesus pointed him to the truth. Write verse 36:

Read Matthew 26:47–54. If Jesus had asked the Father, He would have immediately sent "more than twelve legions of angels." Six thousand soldiers comprised a legion, so Jesus only had to say the word and more than seventy-two thousand angels would have been sent to His aid! The building with the greatest capacity for holding a huge number of angels that my brain can envision is a sports arena. (Jesus is probably cracking up at my tiny imagination!) Picture a big sports stadium filled to the max—that's how many angels would have come immediately to help Jesus. The authority of Jesus is more powerful than our human mind can imagine.

Apparently, Pilate couldn't imagine it either: "So you are a king?" Write the beautiful and amazing answer in verse 37:

As I am writing this, the season of Advent leading up to Christmas has just begun. Jesus said, "For this purpose I was born." Every year we celebrate Christmas, we should remember that Jesus was born for the sole purpose of being our King!

Pilate asked, "What is truth?" But then Pilate went to the Jews and said, "I find no guilt in him." I am left wondering what Pilate thought. Did He believe Jesus?

What do you think?

Chapter 18 closes with something interesting. Read verses 39–40. It appears that the Jews had a custom of mercy and grace during the Passover, i.e., granting amnesty to a prisoner during this holiday.[8] In this case, Barabbas, who was guilty of wrongdoing, was released, while the sinless Jesus was not. By going willingly to the cross at Passover, Jesus was about to release us all from our prison of sin. Oh Lord, it seems too good to be true! The sacrifice of Jesus released you and me from the punishment of our sins. *You* were released as a result of this Passover when Jesus died in your place.

> And he withdrew from them about a stone's throw, and knelt down and prayed, saying, "Father, if you are willing, remove this cup from me. Nevertheless, not my will, but yours, be done." —Luke 22:41–42

Closing Prayer: Thank You, Jesus, for Your sacrifice during that Passover so long ago. Help my heart and mind to always remember that You released me, once and for all, from my sins. Remind me of the power of Your Words. Remind me that legions upon legions of angel armies stand ready to fight for Your kingdom. Lord, help my mind grasp not only Your power, but Your unconditional love for me. Lord, help me to submit my will to Yours. I am Your servant, God; show me the way in which I should walk. In Jesus' mighty name I pray. Amen.

FULFILLING SCRIPTURE

Read John 19 in your Bible.

So much of what you just read in this chapter was prophesied in the Old Testament. I know that the Lord can do amazing and wondrous things, but I am repeatedly in awe of the fact that different people, hundreds of years before it happened, wrote about the crucifixion of Jesus!

I know it's a lot of reading for one day, but I believe the Holy Spirit can do more with these Scriptures than I could ever dream. Pore over Isaiah 53:1–12 and write anything you think shows a link between Isaiah's prophecy and Christ:

Now study Psalm 22:16–31 and write what connects David's psalm to Christ:

Does it amaze you how much Isaiah and David matched the details in John 19? Why do you think God inspired Isaiah and David to write of Christ's sacrifice hundreds of years before it would take place?

When I think of how the Lord sets this all before us, thousands of years later, my heart usually hurts a bit for Austin. God knows all, and He knew that Austin would die after just three years and ten days. Oh, how that hurts my mama heart!

I'm not sure what I would have done if I had known, but it always strikes me that God knew and He didn't stop it. But then my heartache is often soothed by the awesome sovereignty of our God. I see His loving presence and guiding hand in the words of Isaiah and David, even while I cry over the treatment of our Savior in John 19. Somehow, knowing deep in my soul that God is controlling everything by His loving hand helps my grieving heart get some peace. He's got this. He will make things right. Someday. Somehow. Meanwhile, we wait and do our best to show others the truth of Jesus.

Let's turn our attention to the words spoken by Christ in this chapter. First, Pilate did just about everything he could to release Jesus. In what seems like frustration, Pilate came back to question Jesus again, but Jesus did not answer him (vv. 1–9). Pilate's exasperation (v. 10) seems to go through the roof: "You will not speak to me? Do you not know that I have authority to release you and authority to crucify you?" I can almost hear the indignation in Pilate's voice! Other accounts, however, say that Pilate was "amazed" by Jesus' silence (Matthew 27:14; Mark 15:5). John's gospel is the only one to capture what Jesus said in response to Pilate. Write verse 11:

Read Romans 13:1–7 and summarize the main idea in your own words:

The response to Pilate in John 19 and the verses in Romans 13:1–7 circle back to the sovereignty of God. We are governed by our elected political leaders, though all things are ultimately controlled by God. "The king's heart is a stream of water in the hand of the LORD; he turns it wherever he will" (Proverbs 21:1).

Write one thing that is happening in our country right now that frustrates you:

Take a moment and acknowledge the Lord's complete control over the situation. Acknowledge that God alone decides who gets elected, who holds office, who makes our laws, and who governs this country. Bow down in submission to God's authority, which includes our government. Commit to praying for our government, our elected leaders, and our president, for they have each been selected by the Lord to be in such positions. Pray for the Lord to turn their hearts like water in His hand to give God glory by honoring and obeying His commands.

Next, read verses 25–27 in John 19. Please don't miss the fact that in His darkest hour, Jesus thought of His mother, Mary. Jesus asked His beloved disciple to care for her. This is a tender moment because Jesus looks into the crowd and sees His mom and His friend standing together. He wants them to care for each other: "Behold, your son!" and "Behold, your mother!" I can't help noticing, however, that Jesus spoke to His mother first, asking her to care for John. Oh, what a special relationship these two men must have had for Jesus to ask that John take His place as Mary's son!

This moment also speaks to me as a grieving mom. It helps me see that Jesus understands my grief. When Austin died, I needed to hold my younger son, Ethan, so much. I needed to hug him, hold him, touch him, smell him, and be around him because my heart ached for Austin so badly. I think Jesus placed John as Mary's son because He knew how her grieving mother's heart would feel. Jesus knew Mary would suffer a hole in her heart, but He asked John to step into that gap and help His mom. It makes me cry every time I read it. Thank You, Jesus, for understanding my pain. Thank You, Jesus, for interceding for women with broken hearts! Whatever shape the hole in your heart takes, turn to Jesus to help you fill it. He will make a way to get through the pain.

Next, Jesus fulfills another prophecy by saying, "I thirst." Psalm 69:21 says, "and for my thirst they gave me sour wine to drink."

Write John 19:30 below:

Recall that John is the only apostle the Bible says was standing at the cross with the women who followed Christ. The gospel of John also is the only one to capture these words: "It is finished!"

If you recall Psalm 22, it also ends with a similar phrase. Psalm 22:31 says, "He has done it." Notice also that Psalm 22:31, like the prayer in John 17, points to future believers: "to a people yet unborn . . . he has done it."

The other gospels say that Jesus cried out and committed His spirit (Matthew 27:50; Mark 15:37; Luke 23:46). Psalm 31:5 says: "Into your hand I commit my spirit; you have redeemed me, O LORD, faithful God." When Jesus committed His spirit, He fulfilled another prophecy from David's psalms. He also redeemed, or ransomed, you!

When you accepted Jesus as your Savior and Lord, you were ransomed. You were born again. Your salvation was performed. It is finished—hallelujah!

> And [Jesus] said to them, "O foolish ones, and slow of heart to believe all that the prophets have spoken!" —Luke 24:25

Closing Prayer: Father God, thank You for loving me so much that You called me to faith in Jesus as my Savior and Lord. Thank You for being willing to fulfill the Scriptures and die in my place, taking all my sins away. Glory, praise, and honor all belong to You! Your Word amazes and humbles me. Help me live in a manner that shows others the sovereignty of Your love. Help me to always trust that You have a plan that is good. In Jesus' name I pray. Amen.

DO NOT BE UNBELIEVING, BUT BELIEVING!

Read John 20 in your Bible.

It may be difficult or painful to imagine, but try to envision a loved one's grave. Imagine that you just laid your loved one to rest the day before. Worse, imagine you watched as your loved one was tortured, mocked, and forced into an agonizing death. You are exhausted. You are numb. You blindly go to the gravesite because you simply don't know what else to do. But when you arrive, the site is dug up . . . and empty! You whirl around looking for answers as you start sobbing. It's too much . . .

This was Mary Magdalene in John 20. She runs to Peter and John for help. The men race to the tomb, look inside to see the linen wrappings, and then leave. John says he "saw and believed," but then he and Peter simply go back home. It always puzzles me that they went back to their own homes. Perhaps they needed their own families to share the good news. None of the gospels help us understand this initial reaction, but the disciples clearly get together later that day.

First, however, let's take a moment to treasure what happened on that Sunday morning. Of course, we celebrate and marvel over the resurrection. But I want you to soak in something that is precious: Jesus first appeared to a woman. Mary Magdalene was the first person to see Jesus after the resurrection. God chose a woman to be the first to fully understand and experience the joy of Jesus!

Just moments before Mary Magdalene saw Jesus, Peter and John were standing right there by the tomb. Yet Jesus let them look and leave. Jesus waited until only Mary Magdalene was at the tomb. Why did He wait? Why didn't He show Himself to

Peter and John? Why did Jesus choose this woman to be the first to see Him?

Let's marvel at the Lord together. First, angels appeared to Mary Magdalene (read verses 11–14). Write what Jesus said to Mary Magdalene when she was left alone, weeping at the tomb. Write verse 15:

Notice that Mary was so distraught that she didn't recognize Jesus. She thought Jesus was the gardener! Jesus had to say her name, "Mary." Then she finally saw Jesus: "Teacher!"

Write verse 17:

Notice that Jesus also assigned a woman to be the first person to spread the good news! Jesus sent Mary Magdalene to tell the others that He would ascend to the Father. I love the way Jesus said He was ascending "to my Father and your Father, to my God and your God." In this one simple verse, Jesus captured the reconciled relationship between believers and God. The veil was torn and His Father was our Father! Our relationship with God was restored—Praise Jesus!

Later, when all the disciples gathered, Jesus appeared to them. Write the first words Jesus said to His disciples after His resurrection (verse 19):

Next, Jesus showed them His hands and His side, and the disciples "were glad when they saw the Lord" (v. 20). Remember John 16:22 when Jesus said, "So also you have sorrow now, but I will see you again, and your hearts will rejoice, and no one will take your joy from you." The disciples finally understood and rejoiced.

Write what happened next in verses 21–22 of John 20:

Once again we see the power of the very breath of God. Verse 22 says that Jesus breathed on the disciples to give them the promised Holy Spirit. Recall the many references and promises regarding the Holy Spirit we studied in chapters 14–16. All those words spoken by Jesus were true and He was reminding them of His promise. The power of the Holy Spirit, however, was not actually bestowed on the disciples until Pentecost, after Jesus left them and ascended to the Father.[9]

Write verse 23:

Turn back to John 14 and write verse 12:

Recall that in Week 2, Day 2, I asked you to write what you thought John 14:12 meant (page 56). Look back and see what you wrote. In Matthew 16:19, Jesus told the disciples, "I will give you the keys of the kingdom of heaven, and whatever you bind on earth shall be bound in heaven, and whatever you loose on earth shall be loosed in heaven." Jesus was telling the disciples that they had the authority of Christ. He was encouraging them to be bold in their new assignment to spread the gospel and preach the salvation and forgiveness of Christ.

Have you heard the phrase "don't be such a doubting Thomas"? This characterization comes from John 20:24–25. Thomas, one of the original disciples, was not present the first time the Lord appeared and spoke to them. When the others told Thomas, he said that unless he could touch the resurrected Jesus himself, "I will never believe." I couldn't help noticing that Thomas was making a conscious choice: "I will never believe." He was choosing to doubt his friends. He took a stubborn stance.

The next time Jesus appeared to the disciples, however, Thomas was in the room. Fill in the blanks to verses 26–29 below:

Eight days later, his disciples were inside again, and Thomas was with them. Although the doors were locked, Jesus came and stood among them and said, "_____."

Then he said to Thomas, "Put your finger here, and see my hands; and put out your hand, and place it in my side. _____."

Thomas answered him, "_____!"

Jesus said to him, "_____."

Do not be unbelieving, but believing. Blessed are those who have not seen and yet believe. Sisters, that is us! We have not seen Jesus and yet we believe. We are truly blessed. Whatever else happens in your life, you are blessed because you believe in Jesus. No matter how difficult life can be, you have been blessed with belief in Christ. You are not a doubting Thomas. You did not remain stubborn ("I will never believe"), but rather you made the choice to believe in Christ. Praise the Father!

Read 1 Peter 1:8. Those who have not seen Jesus, but still love Him and believe Him, will "rejoice with joy that is inexpressible and filled with glory." Earlier in this study, I asked whether you were filled with joy. I asked whether things of this world were stealing your joy (page 128). It is clear from the Bible that Jesus intended for you to have "inexpressible joy." You had to make a choice to follow Christ, even though you've never seen Him. Will you also make the choice to have "joy that is inexpressible"? I believe joy is the blessing Christ stands ready to pour out on us every day. We just need to walk through each day remembering that we are already blessed because we believe in Jesus.

It is not easy, especially on days when grieving sneaks up on me, but I try to approach difficult days by remembering that God didn't have to draw me to Him, but He did. I try to remember that, although my heart is broken and aching, Jesus suffered and died on the cross so that I could have eternal life surrounded by His glory. Then I make myself repeat a combination of Romans 8:18 and James 4:14: this life is but a vapor, this pain is short, only a mist. The hard stuff in this life is nothing in comparison with heaven and the eternal glory that is waiting for me!

What is a verse that will help you stay focused on the inexpressible joy of being a Christ follower? Write it out and keep it with you.

> "Let not your hearts be troubled. Believe in God; believe also in me."
> —John 14:1

Closing Prayer: Oh Father, thank You for drawing me to Christ! You are so amazing and kind to me. Help me remember that You place high honor on women and that you value my role in spreading the good news. I pray that I will see Your guiding hand in my life and feel the power of the Holy Spirit. Lord, fill me up with Your inexpressible joy. I pray that others will feel my joy in Christ every day. Father, help me to choose joy, even on those days when it is difficult. Holy Spirit, rise up in me and fill me with divine joy that spills over onto others and shines a light on Jesus! In Jesus' name I pray. Amen.

ARE YOU READY TO LOVE OTHERS?

Well, I hope you saved some energy for this final chapter in our study because John concludes his gospel with powerful truths for every believer. Read John 21 in your Bible.

I love how our study begins and ends in the same three themes! First, just as in chapter 13 when Jesus washed the disciples' feet, we see the Lord serving them. He is on the beach, with a fire lit and breakfast started. John 21:13 says that Jesus took the bread and fish and gave it to the disciples, serving them breakfast after a long night of fishing.

Second, blessings flow from obedience. Recall that in chapter 13, Jesus told the disciples that His humble service of washing their feet was an example for them to follow: "blessed are you if you do them" (John 13:14–17). In this final chapter, Jesus appeared and told the disciples to throw their nets on the right side of the boat. Instead of arguing (they had been fishing all night and caught nothing), they threw the net over the right side and hauled in so many fish they had to drag in the net! And don't you love how specific God's Word is? John 21:11 tells us their net held 153 fish and didn't tear!

Third, we are to love others in order to build the kingdom of God. In chapter 13, Jesus told the disciples that it was their love for one another that would point others to Christ: "By this all people will know that you are my disciples, if you have love for one another" (John 13:35). In chapter 21, Jesus told Peter three times that if Peter loved the Lord, he would care for God's people (John 21:15–17).

Let's take a closer look at how the Lord prepared His disciples through these final words. Write verse 5:

This simple verse brings me so much comfort. First, Jesus considers us His children. Sometimes that simple fact still amazes me. Imagine the love between a parent and child, and then imagine such love in a perfect and pure way. Jesus loves you like a daughter. He loves you in complete perfection and purity. If only we could rest in the knowledge of that truth every single day! Second, notice how Jesus already knows the problem the disciples faced through the night. He knew that they did not catch any fish. Jesus knows our problems, our hurts, our difficulties.

Read verse 6 again. Jesus provides. He provides not only what we need that day, but He provides the answers to our problems. The disciples had a problem—an entire night of fishing, but no fish. Jesus had an answer—do as I say and you will be blessed. Jesus knows what we need and He gladly provides in abundance.

Notice also that the disciples, although many were fishermen, could not catch any fish without Jesus! In Week 3, Day 1 (page 87), you wrote about something you might be trying to accomplish apart from God. This scene regarding the disciples reminds us that we cannot do this life alone. We need Jesus!

In verses 15–17, Jesus publicly restored Peter among the disciples. Remember in chapter 13, Peter boldly told Jesus that he would follow Him anywhere, even to death (John 13:37). But Jesus told him, in front of the others, "Will you lay down your life for me? Truly, truly, I say to you, the rooster will not crow till you have denied me three times" (John 13:38). Here, in this third appearance with the disciples, Jesus gave Peter three chances to tell the Lord that he loved Him—one for each time Peter denied knowing Jesus just days before. Fill in the blanks below for verses 15–17 in John 21):

When they had finished breakfast, Jesus said to Simon Peter, "Simon, son of John, _____ ?"

He said to him, "Yes, Lord; you know that I love you." He said to him, "_____ ."

He said to him a second time, "Simon, son of John, _____ _____ ?"

He said to him, "Yes, Lord; you know that I love you." He said to him, "_____ ."

He said to him the third time, "Simon, son of John, _____ _____ ?"

Peter was grieved because he said to him the third time, "Do you love me?" and he said to him, "Lord, you know everything; you know that I love you."

Jesus said to him, "_____ ."

The first time Jesus asks Peter if he loves Him, Jesus says, "Do you love me more than these?" Remember that Peter was a fisherman by trade before Christ entered his life, and in this scene is casting his nets again. It is likely Jesus was referring to Peter's fishing business (the fish, the net, the boat) when He asked if Peter loved Him "more than these." If we love Christ and intend to serve Him alone, it's likely we will have to leave some of our "old" life behind.

Write what you had to leave behind in order to love Christ and serve Him:

It is also possible that the "more than these" Jesus was asking Peter about meant whether Peter thought he loved Jesus more than the other disciples loved Jesus. Recall in chapter 13 how Peter boldly declared he would never leave Jesus, even unto death. Yet, within hours, Peter denied three times even knowing the Lord. Here, perhaps Jesus was giving Peter a chance to repent of his past arrogance and pride and show his spiritual growth. Instead of telling the Lord, "Yes, of course I love You more than these other men!" Peter simply says that he loves the Lord. He has been humbled.

Perhaps the Lord was giving Peter the chance to show he now had the humility to lead the others and have a key role in spreading the gospel.

By the third time Jesus asks "do you love me?" Peter is grieved. Once again, I can relate to Peter. I can almost see him hanging his head after the Lord asks a third time. Peter may have been dragging around his past mistakes and it may have blinded him to the work Jesus was trying to do in his life at that moment: Jesus was likely giving Peter an opportunity to let go of the three denials by asking him three different times, "Do you love me?"

I call this concept of hanging on to past mistakes the "coulda, shoulda, woulda" bucket. The "coulda, shoulda, woulda" bucket holds our past regrets and the weight of guilt. Not letting go of your mistakes is like dragging a big metal bucket filled with stones, scraping around behind you on a long, heavy chain. Can you see that Peter may be dragging his "coulda, shoulda, woulda" bucket into this new situation? We don't know why Peter was grieved by the third "do you love me?" but I think it is possible that Peter was sitting by that fire thinking about the third time he denied knowing the Lord and then hearing that rooster crow. If Peter had taken a moment to get out of his own head and think about the fact that Jesus was the one asking the question for the third time, maybe Peter would not have been "grieved."

If Peter would have considered all the times he had seen Jesus act in love, offer forgiveness, or reach out in compassion, perhaps he would have realized that his sorrow for the denials and his love for the Lord were enough to restore his relationship with Jesus. If Peter had left his "coulda, shoulda, woulda" bucket behind, he might have felt the light of forgiveness offered by Christ. Instead of being grieved by the third "do you love me?" perhaps Peter could have recognized that Jesus was offering a love gift—complete restoration and acceptance.

If you are still dragging around your own "coulda, shoulda, woulda" bucket, reread John 21:15–17 and hear Jesus ask you, "do you love me?" If you answer "yes, Lord!" then know that Jesus has completely restored and accepted you. If you have asked Jesus for forgiveness for whatever sins you carry in your bucket, and you want to turn away from those sins, then Jesus has washed you clean. Jesus has dumped out your bucket. Now leave your "coulda, shoulda, woulda" bucket behind and live in the freedom of Christ.

Next, notice that Jesus told Peter to "feed my lambs" and "tend my sheep" and "feed my sheep." If you love the Lord, your response should be to serve His people. We could pick apart the Greek words for "tend" and "feed" and try to figure out why the Lord used "lambs" and then "sheep," but while I find that kind of word study fascinating (big word nerd!), we might miss the point. Each time Peter answered that he loved Jesus, Jesus pointed to caring for others. Essentially, Jesus was saying, "If you love Me, love others."

And there we are—right back to the beginning of our study: if we love Jesus, we will follow His command to love one another. The simplicity of what God desires of us is astounding. He just wants us to love Jesus and serve others.

The very last words of Jesus recorded in John's gospel drive home this simple message. Read verses 19–21 again. Next, write verse 22, the very last words of Christ in our study:

Jesus told Peter not to worry about what might happen to John in the future, but simply reminded Peter, "You follow me!" All the Lord asks of us is to follow Him. We simply need to keep our hearts focused on Jesus, not worrying about others. As women, I think this is especially true. Like Peter, we tend to compare ourselves to others. I heard once that little girls begin comparing themselves to other little girls by age six or seven. Doesn't that just make you sad?

Yet how often do you compare yourself to someone else? Also, as women, we tend to multitask and pile a lot into our lives. But Jesus reminds us with these words: "You follow me" to remain focused on Him.

Can you think of anything that gets in your way of following Jesus with your whole heart? Maybe it's a giant to-do list. Maybe it's past regrets. Maybe it's people-pleasing. Maybe it's comparisons. Write what you think might be getting in your way of following Jesus more wholeheartedly:

Next, turn back to Week 1, Day 2 (page 25), where you wrote about what you could do to serve others in love. Write it again here:

If you can remove those things that block you from serving Jesus with your whole heart, and you serve others in love, you've done it, my friend! You've obeyed the last words of Christ: "You follow me!"

I love how John finished his gospel so much that we cannot finish this study without taking a moment to consider these last words. Write verse 25:

If John had written all the things Jesus did, even the world could not contain the books that would be written! Isn't that beautiful? Even in his old age (the likely time of his life when John wrote this gospel), you can still feel that John was amazed by Jesus. Oh Lord, it is my deepest prayer that I never lose my sense of awe for our God and my sense of wonder over His Word!

> "I do as the Father has commanded me, so that the world may know that I love the Father." —John 14:31

Closing Prayer: Jesus, You know that I love You. Lord, let my eyes and my heart always follow You. You are amazing and wonderful, deserving of our praise and our heartfelt service. Lord, help me love others as You would. Help me see others with Your eyes and serve them with Your heart. Remove distractions from my life and my heart, Father God. Let my heart be filled with Jesus. Lord, let His last words be wisdom in my heart. Write them on my mind, place them in my heart, and put them on my lips. Lord, let the words of Jesus rule and reign in my life. In Jesus' name I pray. Amen.

WEEK 6 | DAY 5

REVIEW, REFLECT, AND PRAY

Before you begin today, ask God to reveal anything you may have missed the first time through the lessons. Take time to review the verses for each day. Ask God and the Holy Spirit to grant you understanding for His Word. Next, read what you wrote in the lessons and take a few minutes to pray about what God wants you to learn.

If God revealed something to you this week, write about it here:

If God reminded you of something you've been forgetting lately, or showed you something that hasn't been part of your life for a while, write about it here:

If God challenged you to make a change in your life, how did He do it and what change will you make?

Before you end this week, take a few moments to be quiet and still. Take time to let the lessons of this week become wisdom in your heart. Ask the Lord how He wants you to shepherd His flock.

> And he will stand and shepherd his flock in the strength of the LORD, in the majesty of the name of the LORD his God. And they shall dwell secure, for now he shall be great to the ends of the earth. And he shall be their peace. —Micah 5:4–5

Closing Prayer: Father, I praise Your holy, powerful name. Thank You, Jesus, for fulfilling the Scriptures. I give You glory as Shepherd of the kingdom of God. Thank You, Lord, for calling my name and adding me to Your flock. You are indeed great to the ends of the earth. Help me see Your glory and Your kingdom on earth. Help me see how You would have me feed Your lambs, shepherd Your sheep, and tend Your sheep. Show me my purpose, O Lord, and guide my every step, O Holy Spirit! Lead me by the power of the breath of Jesus. I pray that these last words of Christ would impact my life so that I may bring others into Your flock. In Jesus' name I pray. Amen.

DISCUSSION GUIDE | WEEK SIX: JOHN 18-21

HIS FINAL WORDS

1. Review the lessons and what you wrote for Day 5. Share insights with the group.

2. Have you ever experienced the power of God's words? Do you think that you've ever been bowled over by the very breath of God? Tell the group about it.

3. How did tracking the fulfillment of the Old Testament Scriptures fill you with wonder this week?

4. Did you realize that Jesus chose a woman to be first to see Him and realize that He was raised from the dead? Did you know that Jesus first told a woman to spread the good news? How does this knowledge affect you?

5. What actions will you take to tend His sheep? What are you already doing to take care of God's people? Is there anything you plan to do in the future in response to this study?

6. Gather prayer requests for the week and close in prayer.

taking it to the next level

You did it!

This week the goal is to take this study to the next level. It is time to review what we learned and get practical. I find that we often finish one Bible study and then plunge right into the next one. But Bible study is not meant for "head knowledge," or for us to simply learn more verses of Scripture. Bible study is meant to change us, change our lives, and change the lives of others.

My heartfelt desire is that you would use this study to make *two* changes in your life. In order to do that, you must seek the Holy Spirit in your homework this week! Don't stop now—you are almost finished. This is, perhaps, the most important week of all. This week, you will ask the Father, the Teacher, to give you guidance and direction. After studying the verses in such detail, it's important that we step back and get an overview of everything we covered if we want the lessons to stick in our lives. It is time to take note of what we learned and ask our Teacher to show us how to use it. I am praying for you!

WEEK 7 | DAY 1
JOHN 13 AND 14

In your Bible, look at John 13 and 14. Did you underline anything? Did you make notes in the margin? If yes, summarize what you noted here:

Next, go through each lesson in Week 1—John 13, and Week 2—John 14. Note anything that especially struck you:

Considering John 13 and 14, write at least one thing you could do differently as a result of studying the last words of Christ:

Consider what you wrote for the Reader Challenge at the end of Week 1 (page 42). Could you serve in love?

JOHN 15 AND 16

In your Bible, look at John 15 and 16. Did you underline anything? Did you make notes in the margin? If yes, summarize what you noted here:

Next, go through each lesson in Week 3—John 15, and Week 4—John 16. Note anything that was especially influential for you here:

Considering John 15 and 16, write at least one thing you could do differently as a result of studying the last words of Christ:

JOHN 17

In your Bible, look at John 17. Did you underline anything? Did you make notes in the margin? If yes, summarize what you noted here:

Next, go through each lesson in Week 5, chapter 17. Note anything that especially made an impact on you here:

Considering the final prayer of Jesus in chapter 17, write at least one thing you could do differently as a result of studying the final prayer of Christ:

WEEK 7 | DAY 4

JOHN 18–21

In your Bible, look at John 18–21. Did you underline anything? Did you make notes in the margin? If yes, summarize what you noted here:

Next, go through each lesson in Week 6, chapters 18–21. Note anything that was especially influential for you here:

Considering chapters 18–21, write at least one thing you could do differently as a result of studying the last words of Christ:

REVIEW, REFLECT, AND PRAY

As you looked back through the study this week, choose three things that had the most impact on your spiritual walk with the Lord:

Review what you wrote in each day's homework this past week as the one thing you would change as a result of studying the last words of Christ. Write each one again:

1.

2.

3.

4.

Spend the rest of your time asking the Holy Spirit to reveal what He would have you take away from this study. Journal your thoughts here:

TAKING IT TO THE NEXT LEVEL

1. Discuss the things that had an impact on your heart during this study and your four changes. By now, I hope you know each other well enough to share openly and honestly.

2. Discuss what you wrote for the Reader Challenge to serve in love (page 42). Consider whether you could pair up or connect with the women in your group to take on a service project so you can serve in love together.

3. Get in pairs or smaller groups and help each other identify two of the four changes as priority. Write some ideas for how to implement those two changes in your life. Also, note the verse(s) from John 13–21 that inspired the change, and consider committing those words to memory.

4. Decide if you will continue to meet (or perhaps communicate regularly online) in these pairs or smaller groups in an effort to continue to grow together and make those two changes in your life.

5. Get index cards. Each person will need two cards, one for herself and one for her partner/small group. Write your two "priority" changes on your own index card. On the other side, write the verses from John chapters 13–21 that inspired these desired changes. Next, on the other card, write the partner/small group names, telephone numbers, email addresses, and list the two changes each person marked as "priority." Use these cards to pray for your partner, and contact your partner/small group to encourage her/them in making those "priority" changes!

NOTES

1. W. Barclay, *The Gospel of John, Vol. 2* (Philadelphia: The Westminster Press, 1956), 139.

2. http://www.biblegateway.com/resources/ivp-nt/Jesus-Predicts-His-Betrayal.

3. Ibid.

4. Barclay, 148.

5. A fine work on this topic is *Seated with Christ: Living Freely in a Culture of Comparison* by Heather Holleman. The premise of this book is that since we each have a seat at Christ's "round table" with equal access to Him, we needn't compare ourselves with others.

6. "keep." http://www.merriam-webster.com.

7. Some valuable resources on this topic are: *Warfare Praying: Biblical Strategies for Overcoming the Adversary* and the pamphlet *Spiritual Warfare Prayers*, both by Mark I. Bubeck; *Tony Evans Speaks Out on Spiritual Warfare* by Tony Evans; *Reclaiming Surrendered Ground: Protecting Your Family from Spiritual Attacks* by Jim Logan; *Fervent: A Woman's Battle Plan to Serious, Specific and Strategic Prayer* by Priscilla Shirer.

8. "According to the Mishnah, it was customary for amnesty to be granted a prisoner at Passover." Michael G. Vanlaningham, "Matthew," *The Moody Bible Commentary*, ed. Michael Rydelnik and Michael G. Vanlaningham (Chicago: Moody, 2014), 1510.

9. John MacArthur, The MacArthur New Testament Commentary: *John 12–21* (Chicago: Moody, 2008), 381–82.

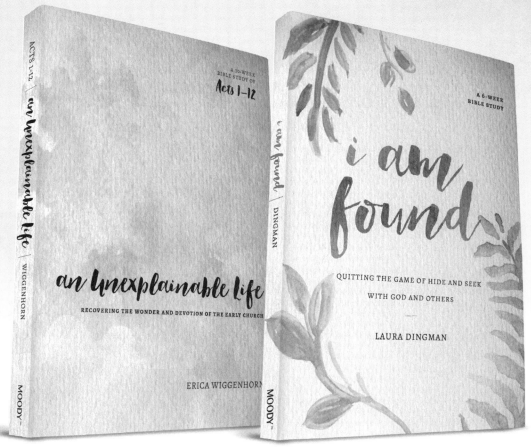